Longman ex-
practice kits

A-level
Economics

Barry Harrison

LONGMAN

Series Editors
Geoff Black and Stuart Wall

Titles available

A-level
Biology
British and European Modern History
Business Studies
Chemistry
Economics
French
German
Geography
Mathematics
Physics
Psychology
Sociology

Addison Wesley Longman Ltd,
Edinburgh Gate, Harlow,
Essex CM20 2JE, England
and Associated Companies throughout the World.

First published 1997

ISBN 0582–31250–7

British Library Cataloguing-in-Publication Data
A catalogue record for this book is available from the British Library.

Set by 35 in 11/13pt Baskerville

Produced by Longman Singapore Publishers Pte Ltd
Printed in Singapore

Contents

Preface

This book is written to help you increase your chances of obtaining a higher grade in A and AS-level Economics or, in Scotland, in Higher Grade Economics. However, it is not just a book of questions and answers, it is really a revision aid. Something designed to help you revise and prepare for your examination.

In preparing this book I have tried to constantly focus attention on those points of good practice that examiners look for in assessing work. I have also tried to encourage the development of those skills such as *analysis* and *evaluation* which must be demonstrated by candidates in order to achieve a high grade. If you can master these skills you are well on the way to success.

This book focuses on those topics most frequently examined at A-level. With the exception of the first and last chapters, each of the chapters follows the same format. The chapters begin with *Revision Tips* which give specific guidance on the topic under review. This is followed by *Topic Outline* which summarises the essential information relevant to each of the topics covered. *Revision Activities* then provide you with the opportunity to test your understanding of the topic and you can assess your progress by referring to the *Answers to Revision Activities*. This section is followed by some *Practice Questions* which it would be useful to attempt before referring to the *Answers to Practice Questions* provided here.

Acknowledgments

In preparing this book I have received a great deal of help and assistance from a variety of people and while I would dearly like to implicate them all in any errors or omissions that the reader finds, as I have not always accepted their advice, I am unable to do so! Nevertheless, I am particularly grateful to Rod Alcock, Peter Maunder and Bob Wright for helpful guidance in preparing the text. I am also grateful to Stuart Wall and to the entire team at Longman. A great deal of the text was written while I was working at the National Institute for Management of the Economy in Baku, Azerbaijan and I am grateful to colleagues there for helpful advice. I must also thank my wife Lea and my children Paul, Matthew and Simon who put up with my long working hours and who are a source of never ending encouragement. Finally I must acknowledge my on-going debt to the late George Stanlake who remains my greatest teacher.

I am indebted to the following Examination Groups for permission to reproduce questions which have appeared in the practice questions and timed practice papers. While permission has been granted to reproduce their questions, the answers, or hints on answers, are solely the responsibility of the author and have not been provided by a group.

Associated Examining Board (AEB)
EdExcel Foundation (London)
Northern Ireland Council for Curriculum, Examinations and Assessment (NICCEA)
University of Cambridge Local Examinations Syndicate (UCLES)
University of Oxford Delegacy of Local Examinations (UODLE)
Welsh Joint Education Committee (WJEC)

How to use this book

This book is designed to guide you through the final stages of your revision in the run up to your A-level Economics examination. It covers the core topics in the A-level Economics syllabuses that are common to all examination boards and some of the other topics which are frequently examined.

The book is arranged in four parts, each dealing with a different aspect of your revision. For the best results it is hoped that you allow yourself sufficient time to read and digest the whole of the book.

Part I   Preparing for the exam

This section of the book offers practical advice and tips to smooth your revision. A Revision Planner is provided to help you to organize your time logically. All teachers know that the essence of success is careful and thorough planning. Advice is given on how to complete the Revision Planner, but again I would stress that you must give yourself plenty of time to work through the whole of your plan. This part of the book also includes a discussion of the different types of question set in A-level Economics papers, and we shall consider the various techniques required to deal with these questions in order to produce the appropriate responses. There is a detailed section on **command** words since failure to interpret these correctly can result in inappropriate responses to quite simple questions.

Part II   Topic areas, summaries and questions

In this part of the book I have identified eight key topic areas (see Chapters 1–8), and for each of these topic areas we shall cover the following aspects:

1 **Key concepts** This is simply a list of the most important terms and concepts associated with the topic under review. You must be familiar with every one of these before you go into the examination.
2 **Revision tips** Here we give specific guidance on revising the particular topic area that we are considering.
3 **Topic outline** This section summarizes the key points of theory/practice in the topic area under review.
4 **Revision activity** The aim here is to provide a check on progress and understanding by making revision an interactive process. Exercises and fill-in questions enable you to assess what you already know and, more importantly, what else you need to know.
5 **Practice questions** This section includes questions of the type used in examining Economics; many are taken from recent examination papers. Guidance on an appropriate response to each of these questions is given in Part III, thus affording you another opportunity to monitor your progress and understanding of the topic.

Part III   Answers and grading

Here you will find answers to the different exercises and questions set in Part II. Some of these answers will be student answers, with examiner comments to help you identify strengths and weaknesses in the answer. Other answers are outline answers constructed by the author to help you identify the points that the examiner would look for in assessing responses to particular questions. It is important to note that the answers given to examination questions are not definitive. For some questions it is possible to adopt a different approach or to bring in points that are equally acceptable.

Part IV Timed practice papers and answers

This part of the book contains questions taken from recent examination papers. The aim here is to give you the opportunity to attempt actual examination questions under examination conditions. In other words, you should attempt these questions within the time limit appropriate to the examination you will take.

The standard time for an essay is 45 minutes, that is, 4 questions to complete within 3 hours in total, as stated on the practice examination paper. Note, though, that the amount of time allocated to each question differs between different examination boards. The 3-hour limit suggested here is a general guide to the pace at which you will have to progress through the paper in order to complete the required number of questions in the examination. For more specific guidance, you must check the regulations of your own examination board.

Again, outline answers are provided so that you can assess your own response against the response an examiner might have been looking for in awarding a high grade.

part I

Preparing for the examination

Planning your revision

I have always felt that revision is very much a personal matter. No one can do it for you and therefore you must use whichever techniques suit you best. Nevertheless, there are certain hints and techniques that are commonly used and which you might find helpful. Do take careful note of the first point, though. It is probably the best advice anybody can give you about your revision!

▶ *Make sure you begin your revision early enough to allow you to cover the whole syllabus. If you rush your revision it is unlikely that you will be able accurately to recall points of detail.*

▶ Plan your revision carefully so that you know exactly what you have to do and when you are going to do it. A detachable Revision Planner is included at the back of this book to help you do this.

▶ When drawing up your revision plan, make sure you organize all material relating to a topic so that it follows a logical sequence. Similarly, make sure your topics are organized in a logical manner. In a different context, Trotski once said, 'Time spent in reconnaissance is seldom wasted'!

▶ Try to revise at the same times each day. Revision will then become part of your daily routine and will be much easier to organize and cope with.

▶ When completing the Revision Planner, set yourself realistic targets. Remember, you are likely to make more progress when you begin revising than when you are near the end of your revision, and some topics will naturally take longer to revise than others. Take care to ensure that your plan allows for this and has some flexibility built into it.

▶ Regularly recap on material you have previously revised in order to ensure that you have not forgotten anything and that your understanding is still clear.

▶ One revision technique you might find useful is to produce a summary sheet containing all of the information you need to know about a particular topic. It is much easier to work from this than it is from your primary set of notes. I also found that producing a summary sheet helped me commit material to memory.

▶ Any student of psychology will tell you that memory works by association. If you know that there are *three* conditions necessary for price discrimination, it is easier to remember what these conditions are.

▶ Refer to past examination papers and examiners' reports to become familiar with how Economics is examined. However, do avoid the temptation to question-spot and never learn an answer by rote in the hope that it will appear on your examination paper.

▶ Revise actively. Regularly test your own understanding, for example by jotting down bullet points which summarize a particular topic, or ask a friend to test your understanding by asking you questions on a particular topic. Practice answering examination questions under timed conditions and check your responses against those provided throughout this book.

▶ Meet regularly with at least one other person taking A-level Economics and help each other to understand points of difficulty. Remember, you are not in competition with each other. There is no reason why you should not both achieve 'A' grades in the examination. After all, no examination board has a fixed limit on the number of 'A' grades it awards at any one time!

Answering examination questions

An important purpose of any examination is to discriminate between candidates, so that the most able candidates obtain the higher grades they merit, while the more limited academic skills and abilities of the other candidates can still be displayed and can be rewarded by the grade they deserve. You should appreciate that examinations are not designed to encourage some candidates to fail: rather, they are intended to enable you to display the skills and abilities that you possess and which, in our case, are appropriate to the subject of Economics.

Skills tested in the examination

So what are these skills and abilities that you need to display in order to obtain a high grade? Clearly, all examinations test the lower-level skills of knowledge and factual recall, which are basically skills associated with memory. However, there are also higher-order skills that enable examiners to discriminate between candidates in awarding marks. These skills are easily summarized, as follows:

▶ **Application** The ability to apply knowledge of economic principles, theories or concepts to data or issues raised in the question. The tendency now is to set questions at 'A' level which allow candidates to demonstrate a broad knowledge of the subject rather than simply a narrow understanding of a single concept.
▶ **Analysis** The ability to break down information into component parts and to identify the assumptions on which a particular line of reasoning depends. For example, being aware of the conditions necessary for a depreciation of the exchange rate to improve the balance of trade.
▶ **Evaluation** The ability to make reasoned judgements about the validity of different arguments. For example, an increase in the money supply is likely to lead to inflation because it will lead to an increase in demand for goods and services.
▶ **Synthesis** The ability to link parts together so as to form a coherent and logical argument that is not obviously apparent before the parts are linked. For example, in analysing the pricing behaviour of a particular firm it is necessary to understand the nature of the market in which the firm operates.

More information is given in the section on command words (p. 6)

Figure P1.1
The pyramid of skills

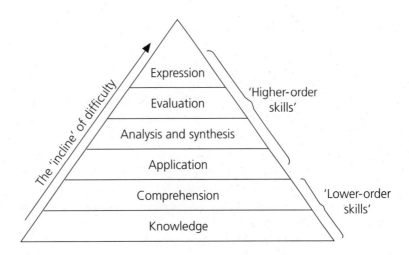

Professor Roy Wilkinson of Sheffield University has illustrated these skills as a pyramid of skills that examinations in Economics at this level try to test (see Figure P1.1). At the base of the pyramid are the lower-level skills of knowledge and factual recall. These are basically skills associated with memory. As we move up the incline of difficulty we have the more demanding skills such as the ability to comprehend and apply economic reasoning to problems. This may sometimes involve the presentation of one or more appropriate and clearly labelled *diagrams*. When you *do* present a diagram make sure that you *use* your diagram in the text to illustrate the points you are making. On other occasions the presentation of *empirical evidence*, such as quoting key points of a particular study, presenting facts or illustrating a point with a practical example, may help to demonstrate these higher order skills.

From the examiner's point of view, a 'good' examination question is one that tests an important and possibly broad area of the syllabus. By this I mean a question which allows candidates to demonstrate a broad knowledge of the subject rather than simply a narrow understanding of a simple concept. The question must also test the different abilities of candidates and discriminate effectively between them in terms of their ability to handle the skills displayed in the pyramid.

All examiners are aware that, as examination papers have evolved, the examination has become more demanding and there is now certainly less emphasis on testing the lower-order skills and much more emphasis on posing questions that allow candidates to display the higher-order skills. This, of course, implies that it is not really possible for candidates to perform well in the essay paper merely by rote learning of notes.

The essay paper

In order to perform well on the essay paper you must demonstrate the skills outlined above. Make sure, therefore, that you are familiar with those skills and that using them becomes part of your writing style. Some additional points to bear in mind include the following:

► Read every question on the examination paper carefully before deciding which questions to attempt. In the tense setting of the examination room it is easy to misunderstand what a particular question is actually asking. To minimize this risk, think as you read the question and decide whether you feel confident about attempting it.

► Decide which questions you will attempt and the order in which you will attempt them.

► Answer first those questions that ask about the topics on which you have the most knowledge.

► Plan your answer before you begin to write. A brief plan only takes a couple of minutes and can save valuable time later by helping you structure your answer more logically. It might also save you from including material which is not strictly relevant to the question you are answering.

► Refer to your plan and the question from time to time to make sure that you are not straying from the issues you need to discuss.

► When you have finished each answer, quickly check that you have not omitted any of the points you intended to include.

► Make sure you attempt the appropriate number of questions. Remember, the first few marks available for any question are much easier to obtain than the last few marks. This is particularly important to remember (and apply) if you are running short of time.

► Throughout your essay, bring in relevant economic theory, and, wherever possible, use relevant examples – particularly up-to-date examples – from the real world to illustrate your points.

► In general, long-winded introductory and concluding paragraphs are inadvisable, partly because of the time constraint and partly because their content is unlikely to tie in with the mark scheme which the examiner will apply in assessing your work. Nevertheless, as we have written above, one of the higher-order skills is the ability to recognize the assumptions on which a particular line of reasoning depends. Thus the first paragraph provides an opportunity for you to define the terms mentioned in the question and to state explicitly any assumptions you are making in the way you have interpreted that question.

▶ Sometimes questions can be interpreted in different ways and, in such cases, one response is neither more correct nor less correct than any other response. As long as you use economic reasoning to answer the question and base your analysis on economic theories, it is possible to score high marks whichever interpretation you have opted for.

The data response paper

There are different types of stimulus-based or data response questions, but all require the same basic approach. Much of what has been written above with respect to the essay paper also applies to the data response paper, though you must remember that the purpose of providing data is to test your understanding of the principles contained in the data. To answer data response questions well, you must therefore base your answer to the question or questions on the data you are provided with. Failure to do this will seriously reduce the mark you are awarded for this paper. Bear the following points in mind:

▶ Data response questions provide a means of assessing whether you can **recognize, understand** and **interpret** economic principles implied in the data you are given. Hence you need to illustrate your points with examples taken from the data whenever it is relevant to do so and to quote directly from the data to reinforce a particular point.

▶ Look for trends and relationships in numerical and statistical data. Where it is relevant to do so, manipulate numerical or statistical data to illustrate trends of economic significance.

▶ Use economic principles to illustrate your points. Search hard for them. They are not always apparent, especially in real-world data.

▶ Try to recognize the limitations of any statistical data you are given or the assumptions on which the conclusions of some extract you are given are based.

▶ Remember that a statistical table is, in effect, an argument. It is therefore necessary to realize that part of what is being tested is your ability to recognize and 'translate' the argument summarized in the table.

The multiple choice paper

The multiple choice paper is designed to ensure that the examination tests as broad a range of knowledge as possible. One objective is to discourage candidates from concentrating on a narrow range of topics in the hope that examination questions will be set on those topics. Thus the multiple choice paper tests breadth of understanding rather than depth. Clearly, factual recall is easily tested by multiple choice questions, but so too are skills of deduction, interpretation and application of economic principles. A good performance in the multiple choice paper can only be achieved by candidates who have a broad knowledge of the subject. Make sure, therefore, that you begin your revision early enough to acquire this. The following points should also prove helpful:

▶ Work quickly, but not so quickly that you do not read the stem of the question *very* carefully.

▶ Try not to do too much in your head. Instead, where you need to, draw diagrams, write down formulae, and so on to help you cope with detail.

▶ It is likely that you will find some questions easier to answer than others, so do not spend too much time trying to answer one question – move on to the next one. Take care, however, that you do not put your response in the wrong place on the answer sheet. Check the question number against the answer number.

▶ Towards the end of the exam, if you have some remaining questions unanswered, have an intelligent guess rather than miss them out.

Command words

Every question on the Economics essay and data response papers will include at least one key word. Such words are known as **command** words. The following is a short guide to the interpretation of some of the most frequently used command words:

▶ **Account for** This word invites candidates to explain the emergence of a particular situation or event. This command word can be interpreted to mean, 'Which economic factors led to . . .'

▶ **Analyse** This word invites candidates to break down an argument or information into component parts and to identify the ways in which these parts are related. It also implies the ability to recognize the assumptions on which a particular line of reasoning depends and the ability to take a critical view of the arguments presented. Note also that if a question asks the candidate to '**Analyse the extent to which** . . .', then it is important to show judgement over the relevant importance of different arguments or events.

▶ **Assess** This word invites candidates to make some kind of judgement on the relative importance of some particular aspect of economics. It is therefore relevant to discuss the influence of other factors or events that influence the topic under review.

▶ **Compare** This word invites candidates to describe two or more situations or activities and, in so doing, to show the *differences* and *similarities* between them. It is therefore not sufficient merely to describe the situations.

▶ **Criticize** or **Critically evaluate** These words invite candidates to present a view on a particular argument, point of view or theory. In any critical assessment a judgement based on the evidence available and the weight of argument is necessarily involved. However, this does not imply that the candidate must be hostile to one line of reasoning and be favourably disposed towards another. A balanced view stressing the relative importance of both issues is acceptable.

▶ **Define** This word invites more than a simple statement of interpretation at this level. In defining a particular concept candidates should also give examples to illustrate it. Where relevant to do so you would be well advised to use appropriate diagrams or formulae and so on to illustrate and elaborate on your definition of a concept.

▶ **Describe** This word invites more than a mere description of some particular economic event or circumstance. Instead a critical review of some particular set of circumstances or events is usually expected.

▶ **Discuss** This word invites candidates to consider a particular statement or set of circumstances. This is an extremely popular command word and it requires candidates to consider the arguments for and against the issue raised in the question.

▶ **Distinguish** This word invites candidates to show that they understand the differences between two (probably frequently confused) concepts. It is essential in distinguishing between concepts that *similarities* and *differences* are discussed and illustrated with appropriate examples.

▶ **Do** or **Does** This word invites candidates to make a judgement on whether one set of circumstances is preferable to another.

▶ **Evaluate** This word invites candidates to make reasoned judgements about the validity of a particular argument or statement. The candidate must therefore present evidence and reasoned argument showing an understanding of all the relevant issues involved.

▶ **Examine** This word invites candidates to unravel the events that led to a particular set of circumstances or the validity of the economic reasoning that underlies a particular point of view. Candidates must stress the relative importance of the different arguments or events mentioned and show their relevance to the basic issue under consideration.

▶ **Explain**   This word invites candidates to interpret the meaning of a particular concept. In such cases, it is always useful to give an example to illustrate understanding of the concept being explained.

▶ **Outline**   This word informs candidates that only a brief description of a particular topic is required. Usually this word is used in the first part of a question for which there is a follow-up part or parts.

▶ **To what extent**   The phrase 'To what extent . . .' implies that there is no definite answer to the question posed. In such cases, the candidate is expected to present both sides of the argument and to exercise judgement by stressing the potency of some arguments over others.

Marking schemes for the essay paper

All examination boards go to a great deal of trouble to ensure that the grade awarded to a candidate does not depend on the examiner who marks the script. As part of this standardization process, examiners follow a mark scheme established before marking begins. The mark schemes currently in use by the examining boards reward different levels of skill displayed by candidates. The following performance criteria, used by the University of London Examinations and Assessment Council, are typical of the approach now adopted by the different boards in assessing the performance of candidates in the A-level Economics examination.

Performance criteria

Grade A
Displays a wide-ranging knowledge of economic principles, concepts and theories together with a sound analysis of issues. Demonstrates an outstanding ability to argue alternative views in order to reach independent conclusions. Shows a thorough understanding of material which is critically evaluated and presented in a relevant, lucid and coherent way, with evidence fully and reliably integrated.

Grade B
Displays a good answer based on knowledge of economic principles, concepts and theories, together with an analysis of the issues involved. Can offer a balanced argument in reaching a conclusion. Shows understanding of material which is evaluated and presented in a relevant way and is supported by evidence.

Grade C
Displays a sound understanding of economic principles, concepts and theories as well as some analysis of issues. Demonstrates the ability to distinguish between differing viewpoints. Shows sound understanding of material, with some ability to evaluate and present it in a way which is appropriate and clear, if at times lacking coherence.

Grade D
Displays some knowledge of economic principles, concepts and theories with an attempt at providing an analysis of alternative views. Shows an understanding of and some ability to evaluate material and to present it with some relevance and coherence.

Grade E
Displays elementary knowledge of well-learned economic facts, but with little awareness of differing viewpoints and limited analysis. Demonstrates some

generalized understanding and some ability to evaluate the material which is presented, but with only partial relevance or coherence.

Grade N

Displays knowledge presented as facts without any awareness of other viewpoints. Demonstrates only limited understanding of material presented, which is insufficiently related to the question. Attempts at evaluating the material are irrelevant and unclear.

Grade U

Contains a few relevant facts but without the development of a clear argument; some examples without any real analysis. Either through complete misunderstanding, continuous or great and repeated errors, uncompensated by any clear answer or, more usually, there is very little substance and is simply scraps of 'general knowledge'.

Markets

✦ KEY CONCEPTS

- ► Capitalism
- ► Centrally planned economy
- ► Demand
- ► Equilibrium
- ► Elasticity of demand (price, income and cross)

- ► Elasticity of supply
- ► Price mechanism
- ► Supply
- ► Total revenue

✓ REVISION TIPS

The operation of markets is a central feature of any course in economics. It is impossible to imagine an examination paper on introductory economics, such as the A-level Economics paper, which does not require a knowledge of supply and demand to answer several questions. Indeed, most examination papers contain at least one question specifically about supply and demand. It is essential, therefore, that you are completely familiar with the nature of these fundamental concepts and the ways in which they interact.

As well as ensuring a sound general understanding of supply and demand, be sure that you can distinguish between the **cause** of a price change and the **effect** of a price change. You must also be able to calculate elasticities and to understand the implications of different elasticities for any change in income or price.

◎ TOPIC OUTLINES

Economic systems

- ► The function of any economic system is to allocate resources to different uses.
- ► One way in which resources can be allocated is through the market. In such cases, the economic system is referred to as **capitalism**.
- ► A different method of allocating resources is through central planning, where the state decides what is to be produced. Economies where this happens are referred to as **centrally planned economies**, because the output of each firm forms part of a master plan for the whole economy.
- ► In practice, economies tend to embrace both features of capitalism and features of planning. Therefore, they are really **mixed** economies.
- ► Economies differ in the extent of state involvement, so that some economies more closely resemble one type of system than that of other economies. Nevertheless, in recent years, *all* economies have tended to push back the frontiers of state involvement and the old, centrally planned economies of the former Soviet Union have been relegated to history.
- ► In market economies, individuals are free within the law to decide what their firms will produce. Since production is undertaken for profit it is said that the **profit motive** guides producers in market economies. This simply implies that producers will produce those goods and services which confer greatest profit.

The price mechanism

▶ The main feature of market economies is a reliance on the **price mechanism** to allocate resources. To see how the price mechanism works, consider a change in consumer preferences so that demand for a particular good increases. As demand rises, price will be pulled upwards. This implies an increase in the profits available from producing that good, and this will encourage firms to produce more. In other words, resources will be reallocated to different uses in response to the changed demands of society. Because changes in consumer preferences lead to changes in the allocation of resources the consumer is said to be **sovereign** in market economies.

▶ As well as providing a **signalling** function, the price mechanism also provides a **rationing** function. When resources are allocated through the market, output is purchased by those who are willing and able to pay the highest prices. In this way, output is rationed on the basis of price to different members of society.

▶ This tells us that market economies are associated with inequality in the distribution of wealth and income.

▶ The main problem with market economies is that of **market failure**. This simply implies that the market fails to allocate resources efficiently. The notion of market failure is considered fully in Chapter 3.

▶ Prices in market economies are determined by the interaction of **demand** and **supply**.

Market demand

▶ In general, there is an *inverse* relationship between the amount an individual demands and the price of the product. For an individual consumer, a theoretical underpinning for this simple observation can be established either by reference to the theory of *diminishing marginal utility* or by using *indifference curve analysis*. (Knowledge of these is not required by all boards. Check your syllabus!)

▶ In this case, what is true for the individual is also true for the market, because the market demand curve simply shows the total amount demanded by consumers at a range of prices.

Market supply

▶ In general, the amount supplied by an individual firm varies *directly* with the price of the product. In other words, as price rises, so the quantity supplied rises, and vice versa. The theoretical underpinning for this belief is given by the *law of diminishing returns*, which explains why, beyond some level of output, costs rise as output rises, so that firms will only supply more as the price of the product rises. Again, what is true for the individual firm is true for the market, i.e. the sum of firms which produce the product. In addition, since some firms are more efficient – that is, have lower costs of production – than others, it is only as the price of the product rises that the less efficient firms will be encouraged to undertake production, as only now will they be able to earn a profit from doing so.

Equilibrium

▶ In a free market – that is, a market where prices are not set by regulation – the price of the product will change until the amount supplied by firms exactly equals the amount demanded by consumers. This unique price, which equates supply with demand, is known as the **equilibrium price**.

▶ Equilibrium is reached through a process of **price adjustment**. For example, if the total amount supplied by firms (market supply) exceeds the total amount consumers demand, there will be a **market surplus**, and in order to dispose of this surplus, firms will be compelled to reduce price. The lower price will

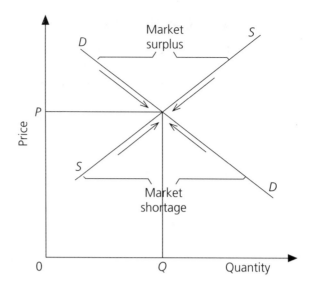

Figure 1.1 The determination of equilibrium in a free market

discourage production but will raise consumer demand until the equilibrium price (OP) is reached, see Figure 1.1. If, on the other hand, demand exceeds supply, there will be a **market shortage** and the existence of this market shortage will drive price upwards. The higher price will encourage production but reduce the amount consumers demand until the equilibrium price OP is reached, see Figure 1.1. In this way, prices in free markets will eventually converge on the equilibrium.

Changes in equilibrium

▶ Once equilibrium is established, there will be no tendency for price (or the amount bought and sold) to change *unless there is a prior change in at least one of the factors affecting demand or supply.*
▶ An **increase in demand** implies that the whole demand curve shifts upwards to the right. In other words, a greater amount is demanded *at each and every price* than previously.
▶ A **decrease in demand** has exactly the opposite effect. The whole demand curve shifts downwards to the left. In other words, a smaller amount is now demanded *at each and every price* than previously.
▶ An **increase in supply** implies that the whole supply curve shifts downwards to the right. In other words, a greater amount is supplied *at each and every price* than previously.
▶ A **decrease in supply** has exactly the opposite effect. The whole supply curve shifts upwards to the left. In other words, a smaller amount is now supplied *at each and every price* than previously.

Changes in demand

A **change in demand** (increase or decrease) can be caused by any one of several factors:

▶ For most goods, **income** and demand are positively related, so that as income rises, demand will increase, and vice versa.
▶ The demand for one good might be affected by changes in the **price of related goods**. In the case of **complements**, a rise in the price of one good will cause a decrease in demand for the complementary good, and vice versa. In the case of **substitutes**, a rise in the price of one good will cause an increase in demand for the substitute, and vice versa.
▶ For some goods there is a **seasonal demand**. In warmer weather, more ice-cream is demanded than in colder weather.

▶ **Tastes** and **fashion** are powerful determinants of demand. When goods become fashionable, demand will increase, and vice versa. This explains why many goods are offered at lower prices in end-of-season sales.

▶ **Advertising** also exerts a powerful influence on demand. When firms advertise their products more heavily, we might expect demand for these goods to increase.

Changes in supply

Similarly, a **change in supply** (increase or decrease) can be caused by any one of several factors:

▶ A change in **costs of production** will have an impact on the market supply curve. For example, if oil prices or wage rates rise, the supply curve will decrease, that is shift upwards to the left (a shift from S_0S_0 to S_1S_1 in Figure 1.2(b)). A rise in productivity would have exactly the opposite effect causing the supply curve to increase, that is shift downwards and to the right.

▶ Over time, **new technologies** will cause an increase in supply.

▶ In the case of agricultural products, **favourable weather conditions** can cause a bumper harvest, which implies an outward movement of the momentary supply curve (see p. 15), and vice versa.

▶ **Taxing** or **subsidizing** a product will have an impact on the supply curve. A change in the rate of VAT (or any other indirect tax) levied on a product will shift the supply curve upwards to the left, whereas granting a subsidy to a product has the opposite effect and shifts the supply curve downwards to the right.

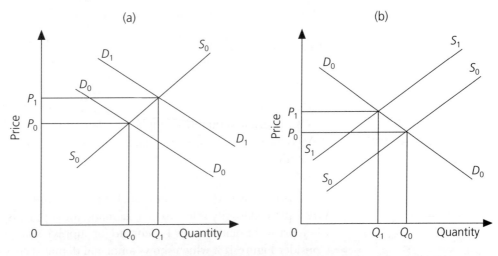

Figure 1.2 (a) The effect of an increase in demand on price and quantity; (b) The effect of a decrease in supply on price and quantity

Changes in quantity demanded and quantity supplied

There is some important terminology that you must be familiar with in order to understand the effect of a **price change**.

With respect to demand, economists distinguish between a **change in demand** and a **change in the quantity demanded**:

▶ A **change in demand** is due to factors already described above and implies a shift of the whole demand curve (see p. 12, changes in equilibrium).

▶ A **change in the quantity demanded** is due to a **change in price** of the product only. This type of change causes a movement along an existing demand curve in one of two ways:

   1 If the price of a product rises then the quantity demanded falls, this is referred to as a **contraction** in demand or a **reduction** in quantity demanded.

   2 If the price of a product falls then the quantity demanded rises, referred to as an **extension** or **expansion** of demand.

Similarly, there is also a difference between a **change in supply** (due to factors described above) and a **change in the quantity supplied**, which again is only ever caused by a **change in price**. A change in price has a direct effect on the supply curve in that:

1 If the price of the product rises then the quantity supplied rises, referred to as an **extension** or **expansion** of supply.

2 If the price of the product falls then the quantity supplied falls, referred to as a **contraction** in supply or **reduction** of quantity supplied.

To understand the **effect** of a price change, it is essential to understand its **cause**. For example, if the price of a product rises, will more or less be supplied when the market returns to equilibrium as compared with the original situation? Consider Figure 1.2 on p. 13.

▶ In Figure 1.2, the market is initially in equilibrium with price at P_0 and with quantity Q_0 supplied and demanded. In Figure 1.2(a) there is an **increase in demand** from D_0D_0 to D_1D_1. As a result, the price of the product rises to P_1 and the equilibrium quantity supplied and demanded also rises to Q_1.

▶ In Figure 1.2(b) there is a **decrease in supply** from S_0S_0 to S_1S_1. As a result, the price of the product again rises to P_1 but, in this case, the equilibrium quantity supplied and demanded falls to Q_1.

The effect of a price change depends on its cause!

Price elasticity

▶ The impact of any price change on the amount demanded or the amount supplied depends on **price elasticity of demand (PED)**, or **of supply (PES)**. Price elasticity is measured in the following way:

$$\text{PED or PES} = \frac{\%\ \text{change in quantity of } X}{\%\ \text{change in price of } X} = \left(\frac{\Delta Q}{Q}\right)\left(\frac{P}{\Delta P}\right)$$

where:

X is the product
Q is the original quantity supplied or demanded *before* the price change;
ΔQ is the change in quantity supplied or demanded as a result of the price change;
P is the original price *before* the change; and
ΔP is the change in price.

▶ When price elasticity is greater than 1, then demand (or supply) is said to be *elastic*. When price elasticity is less than 1, demand (or supply) is said to be *inelastic*, and when price elasticity equals 1, demand (or supply) is said to be *unit elastic*.

▶ Consider Figure 1.3, which shows a normal demand curve for good X. Note that when the equilibrium price of X is £10, then 2,500 units of X are supplied and demanded. Now, for some reason there is an increase in the supply of X (shown by a shift in the supply curve from S_0S_0 to S_1S_1). This increase in supply causes a fall in the price of X and an extension of demand. The new equilibrium price of X is £9, with 3,000 units supplied and demanded. We can use this information to calculate price elasticity of demand (PED) for this change in price.

$$\text{PED} = \left(\frac{\Delta Q}{Q}\right)\left(\frac{P}{\Delta P}\right) = \left(\frac{500}{2,500}\right)\left(\frac{10}{1}\right) = 2$$

Note: Strictly speaking PED is negative in the above example, since change in price, ΔP, is −1. However, this negative sign is usually ignored.

Elasticity of demand and total revenue

There is an important relationship between price elasticity of demand and the total revenue earned by producers of the product, which is easily summarized, as follows:

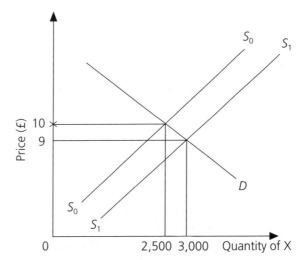

Figure 1.3   The effect of a change in supply on price and quantity

▶ When demand is elastic, a **fall in price** leads to a **rise in total revenue** and a **rise in price** leads to a **fall in total revenue**.

▶ When demand is inelastic, a **rise in price** leads to a **rise in total revenue** and a **fall in price** leads to a **fall in total revenue**.

▶ If elasticity is unitary, a change in price leaves total revenue unchanged.

Consider Figure 1.3 again. We know that when price falls from £10 to £9, demand is elastic. Let us see what happens to total revenue. At a price of £10, the total revenue earned by producers of good X was £10(2,500) = £25,000. When price falls to £9, the total revenue rises to £9(3,000) = £27,000.

Factors influencing price elasticity of demand

Price elasticity of demand is influenced by several factors including:

▶ The greater the **proportion of income** spent on a product, the more elastic demand will tend to be. A 10 per cent rise in the price of cars will have a greater impact on the demand for cars than a 10 per cent rise in the price of a box of matches will have on the demand for matches.

▶ The greater the **number of substitutes** for a product (and the closer these substitutes are to the product), the more elastic demand for that product will tend to be.

▶ The easier it is to **postpone the purchase of a replacement product**, the more elastic demand will tend to be. In the case of consumer durables such as dishwashers, it is often possible to delay replacement, and in such cases a rise in the product's price is likely to have a greater impact on demand than an equivalent price rise for a non-durable good.

▶ If a product is **habit-forming** it will tend to have a lower price elasticity of demand than products which are not habit-forming. Consumers will find it more difficult to respond to a price rise, for example, with a cut in demand.

▶ **Time** is an important determinant of price elasticity of demand. In some cases it is difficult to find substitutes in the *short run*. For example, the demand for oil is more price elastic in the long run than in the short run because if the price of oil rises, then it will take some time before heating systems can be changed, consumers can substitute more cars which burn less fuel, and so on.

Factors influencing elasticity of supply

The main determinants of price elasticity of supply are equally easily summarized:

▶ The **time period** is the most obvious determinant of elasticity of supply. In the **momentary period**, supply is completely inelastic. In the **short run**, however, it may be possible to work the *fixed* factors more intensely by employing more *variable* factors, so that supply is more elastic than in the momentary period. In the **long run**, it is possible to vary the input of *all* factors of production (fixed and variable) so that supply is even more elastic.

▶ The **extent to which costs change as output changes** is also an important determinant of elasticity of supply. When costs rise steeply as output rises, supply will tend to be less elastic than otherwise.

▶ If the product can be **stored** without deterioration, supply will tend to be more elastic than if the product cannot be stored, because it will be possible to increase or decrease stocks in response to a change in price.

▶ If there is **surplus capacity** in the industry, so that firms can readily and easily expand output, supply will tend to be more elastic than if the industry is operating at or near full capacity.

▶ In some industries, there are significant **barriers** to the entry of new firms (see pp. 22, 26–27). In such cases, supply will tend to be less elastic than when there are no barriers to the entry of new firms.

Income elasticity of demand (IED)

▶ Economists are also interested in **income elasticity of demand** (**IED**). This is the responsiveness of demand to changes in income.

▶ For **normal goods**, demand increases as income increases. However, this is not true of all goods. A good is described as an **inferior good** when demand **decreases** as income **increases**. Poor-quality clothing might provide some examples of inferior goods. Most people prefer 'designer' labels and purchase these in preference to other types of clothing as their income rises.

▶ Income elasticity of demand is measured in the following way:

$$\text{IED} = \frac{\% \text{ change in quantity of } X \text{ demanded}}{\% \text{ change in income}} = \left(\frac{\Delta Q}{Q}\right)\left(\frac{Y}{\Delta Y}\right)$$

where:

X is the product
Q is the original quantity demanded *before* the change in income;
ΔQ is the change in demand as a result of the change in income;
Y is the original income *before* the change; and
ΔY is the change in income.

Cross-elasticity of demand (CED)

▶ Economists are also interested in **cross-elasticity of demand** (**CED**). This is the responsiveness of demand for one product to a change in the price of another product. Cross-elasticity of demand for two products, *a* and *b*, can be measured in the following way:

$$\text{CED} = \frac{\% \text{ change in quantity of } a \text{ demanded}}{\% \text{ change in price of } b} = \left(\frac{\Delta Q_a}{Q_a}\right)\left(\frac{P_b}{\Delta P_b}\right)$$

where:

Q_a is the original demand for *a before* the change in the price of *b*;
ΔQ_a is the change in the amount of *a* demanded as a result of the change in the price of *b*;
P_b is the original price of *b before* the change; and
ΔP_b is the change in the price of *b*.

▶ If cross-elasticity of demand is **positive**, then the two products are **substitutes** because a rise (fall) in the price of one product causes a rise (fall) in demand for the other product.

▶ If cross-elasticity of demand is **negative**, then the two products are **complements** because a rise (fall) in the price of one product causes a fall (rise) in demand for the other product.

Note:
▶ Price elasticity of demand (and supply) relate to *movements along* a demand (and supply) curve.
▶ Income and cross elasticity of demand relate to the extent of *shift* in a demand curve.

REVISION ACTIVITIES

1 (a) Apply your knowledge of the price mechanism to explain why strawberries are cheaper in the summer than they are in the winter.
  (b) Earlier, on p. 11, it was suggested that as the price of a product rises, firms will supply more, yet during the summer months more strawberries are available despite the fact that the price of strawberries falls. How can this apparent paradox be explained?
  (c) Is the supply of fresh strawberries available in shops and on the markets likely to be elastic or inelastic? Is the same true of strawberries available from growers?
2 Explain how the price mechanism might be applied to easing the problems of traffic congestion:
  (a) on motorways;
  (b) in city centres.

PRACTICE QUESTIONS

Question 1
Read through the extract below and answer the questions which follow.

Coffee prices

Sainsbury yesterday signalled the end of 10 years of cheap coffee for British consumers by raising the price of its own-brand instant from 89p to 99p. The supermarket chain's move came amid frenzied coffee trading on commodity exchanges throughout the world.

Nestlé, makers of Nescafé, would not comment on the timing of any price increase for the biggest-selling brand in the UK. The Finnish producer Paulig, owner of the Lyons and Melitta brands, said ground coffee will rise in price 'but it will probably not be for some weeks'.

Reports of severe frost damage to Brazilian coffee plantations sent the open-market price of coffee for September delivery spiralling from about $900 (£600) a ton to $4,000 a ton, the highest level since 1986. The price has risen fivefold since January 1993; even before the Brazilian frost reports, the cost had been rising because some farmers, disheartened by low coffee prices worldwide, had moved on to more lucrative crops.

These increases threaten to bring the curtain down on a golden age of cheap coffee for British consumers. Since the winter of 1986/87, the price of a quarter pound jar has fallen slightly – then, Nescafé Gold Blend cost £1.80; now it is £1.56.

Given that the intervening years saw the high inflation of the 1980s boom, the real cost has fallen even more steeply. This, in turn, has propelled a boom in coffee drinking: the sterling value of coffee sold in Britain overtook that of tea

continued

---

continued

eight years ago. Now the prospect is looming of another coffee 'switch-off' comparable to that of the 1970s, when the rocketing prices encouraged a generation of students and young workers away from coffee and on to tea. Some became so fond of the taste that they never switched back and have recently been complaining of the unavailability of after-dinner tea in top restaurants.

    The depressed price of coffee during the last eight years is due to several factors, including the collapse of the International Coffee Agreement in 1989. The agreement had kept coffee prices artificially high: with its demise, supplies flooded the market and the price stayed low.

(Adapted from D. Atkinson, 'Coffee Prices on the Boil',
The Guardian, 12 July 1994)

(a) Using supply and demand analysis, give two reasons why a jar of instant coffee has risen in price. Illustrate your answer with a diagram. [*6 marks*]

(b) Explain why 'it will probably not be for some weeks' before ground coffee prices rise. [*4 marks*]

(c) In the context of the passage, explain the meaning of the statement, 'the real cost of coffee has fallen even more steeply'. [*3 marks*]

(d) Using the concept of cross-elasticity of demand, explain the relationship between coffee prices and the consumption of tea in the 1970s. [*6 marks*]

(e) Examine the economic effects of 'the collapse of the International Coffee Agreement' on the market for coffee. [*6 marks*]

Question 2

(a) In a market economy, prices:
    (i) give signals to participants in the economy;
    (ii) act as a rationing device; and
    (iii) provide incentives.
    Explain *each* of these functions. [*12 marks*]

(b) Evaluate the economic arguments *for* and *against* introducing a system where schools charge their own fees and the government gives parents a voucher for each child which is used to contribute towards school fees. [*13 marks*]

AEB

Question 3

A company which owns a chain of shops hiring out pre-recorded films on video has estimated that the elasticities of demand for the product are as follows:

► The price elasticity of demand is −0.8.
► The income elasticity of demand is +2.8.
► The cross-elasticity of demand with respect to the price of tickets to the cinema is +1.5.

(a) Explain carefully what is meant by each of these figures. [*12 marks*]

(b) Assuming the estimates are correct, discuss the implications for company policy. [*13 marks*]

AEB

2 Market structure and private industry

◆ KEY CONCEPTS

- ▶ Advertising
- ▶ Average cost
- ▶ Average revenue
- ▶ Barriers to entry
- ▶ Cartel
- ▶ Contestable markets
- ▶ Deregulation
- ▶ Kinked demand curve
- ▶ Loss
- ▶ Marginal cost
- ▶ Marginal revenue

- ▶ Monopolistic competition
- ▶ Monopoly
- ▶ Non-price competition
- ▶ Normal profit
- ▶ Oligopoly
- ▶ Optimal allocation of resources
- ▶ Perfect competition
- ▶ Price discrimination
- ▶ Price leadership
- ▶ Privatization
- ▶ Supernormal profit

✓ REVISION TIPS

Theories of the firm are an important part of the syllabus but sometimes appear difficult because of the amount of detail involved. They will seem much simpler if you are familiar with the assumptions of the different models, in which case you can often work out from first principles what will happen in response to some occurrence, or shock, such as a change in demand. Try also to remember how many assumptions are associated with each theory of the firm.

To understand the different theories of the firm, you should also be familiar with the nature of fixed, variable, average and marginal costs of production. Moreover, you must understand the nature of average and marginal revenue: in particular, how they behave as output changes and the way in which they are related.

Also be familiar with the **short-run** time period (at least one factor of production fixed) and the **long-run** time period (all factors variable).

Be clear about the economist's notion of profit and the accountant's notion of profit. Economists frequently refer to the concept of **normal profit**, which is the minimum acceptable level of profit necessary to keep the firm in the industry. In this sense normal profit is often regarded as a 'cost' of production, in that if profit falls below normal, in the *long run*, firms will leave the industry. Accountants have a more mechanistic view of profit, regarding it simply as the difference between revenue from sales and costs of production.

The privatization programme still has some way to run. Make sure, therefore, that you understand the motives for, and consequences of, privatization. However, we are now well into the privatization programme and you should be aware of the ways in which the government regulates the privatized utilities, especially as regards the prices they charge for their products.

TOPIC OUTLINE

Perfect competition

▶ Perfect competition analyses how firms behave when certain conditions are met.
▶ Many of the assumptions on which perfect competition is based can be seen to be very unrealistic in the modern world.
▶ Nevertheless, perfect competition is important because it leads to a particular allocation of resources which is often thought to be ideal or 'optimal'.
▶ The assumptions of perfect competition are easily summarised, as follows:

   – there are many buyers and many sellers, each so small that by their own actions they cannot influence the market price of the product;
   – there is no product differentiation (i.e. a homogeneous product is traded);
   – buyers and sellers have perfect information about the prices charged for the product anywhere in the market;
   – consumers are indifferent from whom they buy;
   – there are no barriers to entry or exit from the industry; and
   – producers aim to maximize profit.

▶ Given these conditions, the firm will be a **price taker**. It is powerless to influence the market price and must take it as given.
▶ This implies that the firm *perceives* its demand curve to be **perfectly elastic** at the ruling market price.
▶ Therefore, the firm sells each unit at the same price, and marginal revenue equals average revenue equals price.
▶ To maximize profit, the firm simply equates marginal cost with marginal revenue.
▶ In the *short run*, the firm might earn **supernormal profit** (i.e. profit in excess of normal profit) or it might make **subnormal profit** (i.e. profit less than normal profit).
▶ The adjustment from short-run supernormal profit to long-run normal profit is shown in Figure 2.1.

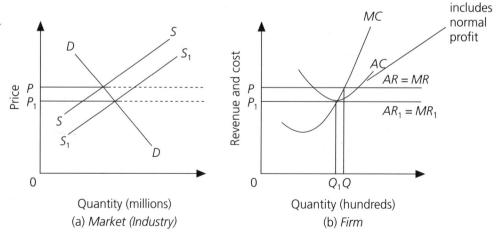

Figure 2.1 The adjustment from short-run supernormal profit to long-run normal profit

(a) *Market (Industry)*

(b) *Firm*

▶ Figure 2.1(a) shows the *market* supply and demand curves for this product. S and D are the initial supply and demand curves, giving an equilibrium market price of OP. Each small firm is a *price taker* with a perfectly elastic demand curve ($AR = MR$) at this price.
▶ Figure 2.1(b) shows the output the profit-maximising firm produces at this price, which is determined at OQ by the intersection of the marginal cost curve and the marginal revenue curve.

▶ In summary, P is the initial market price and the firm produces Q units. Note that when price is P, average revenue exceeds average cost (which includes normal profit) and therefore the firm earns supernormal profit.

▶ The existence of supernormal profit attracts other firms into the industry – remember, there are no barriers to entry – and so market supply shifts to S_1. As supply increases, price falls, until the firm earns only normal profit. In this case, price is P_1 and the firm produces Q_1 units.

▶ At this price and output combination the firm earns only normal profit, and therefore the firm and the industry are in long-run equilibrium.

▶ Note that in long run equilibrium with price at P_1 and output at Q_1, price $= AR = MR = MC = AC$.

▶ If, on the other hand, the initial market price was below OP_1 in Figure 2.1, then the price taking firm ($AR = MR$) would equate MC with MR at an output *less than* OQ_1.

▶ With price $< P_1$ and output $< Q_1$, $AC > AR$ and so the firm makes *subnormal* profit.

▶ Firms cannot go on making subnormal profit or sustaining losses indefinitely and, in the long run, the least efficient firms will be forced to leave the industry (remember, there are no barriers to exit), and so market supply shifts leftwards. As supply decreases, price rises, until the profit-maximising firm earns only normal profit. In this case price is once again P_1 and the firm produces Q_1 units.

▶ At this price and output combination P_1/Q_1 the firm earns only normal profit ($AC = AR$), and therefore both the firm and the industry are in long-run equilibrium.

▶ One point to note from this analysis is that under perfect competition the firm always equates price with marginal cost, so that consumers are charged a price which exactly covers the extra cost of producing the last unit. This is often thought to be an 'optimum' (best possible) allocation of resources.

▶ Another point to note is that in the long-run firms are forced to produce where average cost is at a minimum (the 'technical optimum').

▶ In perfect competition, therefore, it is often argued that resources are allocated optimally and firms produce at their technically most efficient level.

Monopoly

▶ A 'pure' monopoly exists when there is only a single supplier of a product.

▶ The market demand curve is therefore also the firm's demand curve.

▶ In a monopolistic market, marginal revenue does *not* equal average revenue because in order to sell more units the firm is compelled to reduce the price of all units (except in the case of perfect price discrimination).

▶ To maximize profits the firm produces where marginal cost equals marginal revenue. Figure 2.2 illustrates this.

▶ In Figure 2.2, AR is the monopolist's average revenue curve and MR is the associated marginal revenue curve. MC is the monopolist's marginal cost curve and AC is the monopolist's average cost curve.

▶ When the profit-maximising monopolist equates marginal cost with marginal revenue, supernormal profits of $PRST$ are earned.

▶ An important point to note about Figure 2.2 is that the price consumers pay for the last unit they purchase is *greater than* the marginal cost of producing that unit. In other words, consumers value additional units of the monopolist's product more highly than they value alternatives.

▶ Under monopoly, therefore, there is no optimal allocation of resources. Note that as well as price above marginal cost, the profit-maximising output OQ occurs with AC above its minimum achievable level.

▶ Unlike in perfect competition, there is not necessarily any competitive process which results in supernormal profits being competed away.

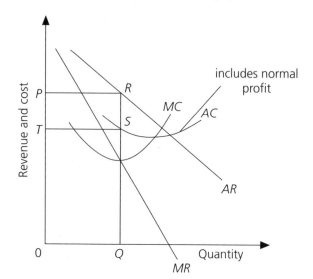

Figure 2.2 Equilibrium price
and output under monopoly

▶ It is possible to preserve supernormal profits in the long run as long as there are **barriers to the entry** of new firms into the industry.

▶ The essence of monopoly power is therefore the ability to restrict the entry of new firms into the industry.

▶ The more complete the barriers to entry, the greater the monopolist's power to earn long-run supernormal profits.

▶ Deregulation has resulted in a reduction in the barriers to entry for many industries. However, one important barrier which still remains is the existence of vast economies of scale, which means that there is often a natural tendency towards the emergence of a single supplier in some industries. Chemicals, oil, gas and electricity are obvious examples.

Price discrimination in monopoly

▶ Price discrimination occurs when a firm charges different prices for the same product. This might be because existing consumers are able to buy additional units at a lower price, or because different consumers pay different prices.

▶ For price discrimination to be possible (and profitable), certain conditions must exist, as follows:

– supply must be controlled by a monopolist;
– consumers who pay the lower price must not be able to resell to consumers who pay the higher price; and
– consumers who pay different prices must face different price elasticities of demand for the product.

▶ Figure 2.3 illustrates one way in which price discrimination might work.

▶ Markets (a) and (b) are two separate markets. The demand curves from these markets are added together to give the 'combined market' demand curve ((a) + (b)).

▶ The problem for the monopolist is to decide how to allocate the product between the two markets in order to maximize profit.

▶ To do this the monopolist equates marginal cost for whole output with the **combined** marginal revenue.

▶ When marginal cost and combined marginal revenue are equal, the output produced (OQ) is then divided between markets (a) and (b) in order to equate marginal revenue in each individual market with marginal cost of producing the last unit.

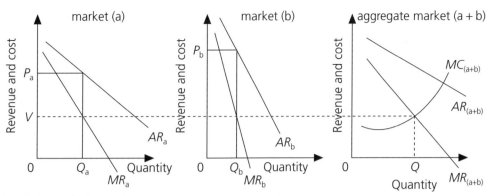

Figure 2.3 Price discrimination under monopoly

▶ In Figure 2.3, this implies a total output of Q which is divided between the two markets, giving a price and output combination of $P_a\,Q_a$ and $P_b\,Q_b$, respectively.

Monopolistic competition

▶ A monopolistically competitive market consists of a large number of producers each supplying a slightly differentiated product.
▶ Product differentiation might be real or imaginary in the sense that firms promote their own brand through **advertising** the unique, but untestable, qualities it possesses.
▶ For example, some washing powders claim to give the 'cleanest, softest, whitest' wash, but it is impossible to define these terms precisely, let alone test to see if they are achieved.
▶ An important assumption of monopolistic competition is that there are no barriers to entry into or exit from, the industry.
▶ Each firm in monopolistic competition has a monopoly over its own brand of the product, and so each firm faces a downward-sloping demand curve for its product.
▶ Because of this, average and marginal revenue diverge, just as they do under pure monopoly.
▶ Figure 2.4 is used to analyse short-run and long-run equilibrium under monopolistic competition.

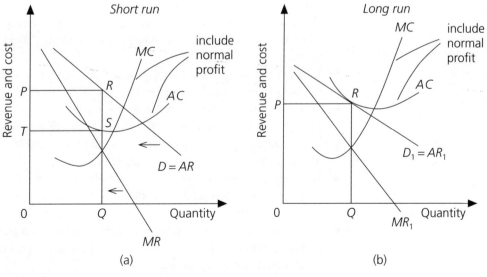

Figure 2.4 The adjustment from short-run equilibrium to long-run equilibrium under monopolistic competition

▶ In Figure 2.4(a), the firm is in short-run equilibrium because it produces where marginal cost equals marginal revenue.
▶ The equilibrium price and output are P and Q respectively, and the firm earns *supernormal profit* of *PRST*.

▶ However, this is not a long-run equilibrium. The existence of supernormal profit will attract other firms into the industry. This will reduce the demand for any individual brands of the product as some consumers are attracted away from existing suppliers by the new, differentiated products now on the market.

▶ We can show the impact of new firms attracting some (but not all) of the firm's customers as a leftward shift (decrease) in the demand curve (*AR*) in Figure 2.4(a) and its associated marginal revenue curve (*MR*).

▶ In addition all firms might now face *increased costs* because of increased competition for scarce resources.

▶ Figure 2.4(b) shows the long-run equilibrium position of the firm in monopolistic competition. The firm produces where marginal cost equals marginal revenue, but now only earns normal profit because average cost equals average revenue.

▶ The fact that the firm earns only normal profit in the long run is the only similarity between monopolistic competition and perfect competition.

▶ In monopolistic competition there is no optimal allocation of resources, because the price consumers pay for the last unit they consume does *not* equal the marginal cost of production.

▶ Note also that although the firm earns only normal profit in the long run, the average cost of production is not pushed to its minimum point, as it is under perfect competition.

▶ This implies that each individual firm operates with excess capacity, and average costs would fall if output was expanded – that is, if there were fewer producers in the industry!

Oligopoly

▶ Oligopoly is sometimes referred to as **competition among the few** because the industry consists of a few large-scale producers.

▶ It is impossible to give a definite answer as to exactly how many producers are necessary for an oligopoly to exist.

▶ However, the main characteristic of oligopoly is **interdependence**, i.e. firms cannot take decisions about price and output without regard to the way rivals will react.

▶ Because of this, it is difficult to say very much about price and output determination in oligopoly.

▶ What we do know is that *prices in oligopolistic markets tend to be relatively stable,* and that when they do change, all producers tend to change their prices by a similar amount.

▶ In general, look at what happens when one bank raises its interest rates or one of the big petrol companies raises the price of its petrol.

▶ Sometimes this pattern of behaviour is not followed and price competition is intense between rival firms. This is referred to as a **price war**.

▶ Price wars are often precipitated by a fall in demand for the industry's product, so that all producers experience falling sales.

▶ For large-scale producers, this is especially important because of the relatively large fixed costs involved in production. Price cutting is an attempt to increase sales.

▶ In the absence of a price war, prices are often set by a **price leader**. In this case, one firm initiates a price change and other firms accept the change and adjust their own prices accordingly.

▶ Price leadership can either be **dominant firm leadership** or **barometric leadership**.

▶ In the case of **dominant** firm leadership, the price leader is the largest supplier, and this firm, because of its size, exerts the greatest influence on output and price. Other firms simply take their cue from the leader.

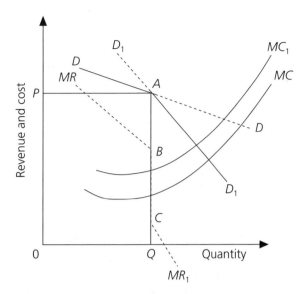

Figure 2.5 Price and output under oligopoly remain unchanged when the marginal cost changes in the region BC when each firm perceives its demand curve to be kinked at the ruling market price

▶ In the case of **barometric** price leadership, the leader is the firm that most accurately interprets changes in demand or supply for the product. This may well be a small firm which is close to the market 'players'. Again, this is accepted by other firms in the industry, who simply emulate changes initiated by the leader.

▶ Price leadership might explain price stability in oligopolistic markets. After all, frequent price changes increase firms' costs and are therefore not implemented lightly.

▶ However, a different explanation of price stability is given by the **kinked demand curve**. The basic idea is that if a firm *raises its price*, other competitors will not retaliate. Instead, they will leave their own prices unchanged so that consumers will switch to the lower-priced substitutes they now offer, thus raising their market share.

▶ The situation is different in the case of a *price reduction*. If one firm lowers price, other suppliers will lose sales to this firm, and to avoid this, they are certain to match a price cut. The implications of this are explained by reference to Figure 2.5.

▶ In Figure 2.5, the firm's demand curve is *perceived* to be **kinked** at the ruling market price, *P*. If the firm raises its price, it will do so in isolation. For a *price rise*, demand is therefore relatively elastic (segment *DA*). For a *price cut*, there will be retaliation and demand is therefore relatively inelastic for a price reduction (segment *AD*$_1$).

▶ Because of this, the possibility is that firms perceive their demand curve to be kinked at the ruling market price. This is sometimes offered as an explanation for the relative price stability in oligopolistic markets.

▶ However, the model has another implication. Because the demand curve is perceived to be kinked at the ruling market price, the firm is simultaneously at a common point A on *two* separate demand curves.

▶ The associated marginal revenue curve will therefore be discontinuous below the kink. Thus marginal revenue will be **indeterminate** at price *P*.

▶ As long as marginal costs rise or fall within the discontinuous region of the marginal revenue curve (*BC*), the firm will have no incentive to adjust price or output since it will still be producing where marginal revenue equals marginal cost.

▶ The kinked demand curve therefore offers a possible explanation of price stability, even when costs of production change!

▶ The kinked demand curve is an interesting idea, but it is not a complete theory of oligopoly since it only tells us *why* price and output, once established, might be relatively stable. It does not tell us *how* price and output are decided in the first place.

Collusive oligopoly

▶ Another explanation of relative price stability in oligopoly is that oligopolists might reach a **collusive agreement**.

▶ The basic idea is that oligopolists set price and output as though they were a single monopoly firm. This establishes the profit-maximizing price and output for the industry.

▶ They then divide the output to be produced between themselves, each firm producing only its allotted quota. Such collusive agreements are known as **cartels**, and OPEC is the most often quoted example of a cartel.

▶ The problem with cartels is that they tend to be unstable. It is in each firm's interest to join the cartel, since it removes them from an uncertain and possibly competitive situation. However, once agreement is reached, each firm has an incentive to secretly undercut the cartel price and sell additional output, thus increasing its own profit above the level projected by the cartel.

▶ If a sufficient number of suppliers undercut the cartel price, profits will fall below the projected level and the cartel might well collapse.

Non-price competition

▶ Although prices are relatively stable in oligopolistic markets, this does not imply an absence of competition in such markets. It simply implies an absence of price competition. **Non-price competition** is therefore common in oligopolistic markets.

▶ One form of non-price competition is **advertising**. Firms differentiate their products and stress in their advertising the 'unique' features of their own product.

▶ Advertising might be either aggressive or defensive. It can be aggressive in an attempt to poach consumers away from rival firms. In this case, the aim of advertising is to increase demand for the firm's product and reduce its elasticity of demand.

▶ However, it can also be defensive, because relatively large advertising represents a barrier to entry. Any potential entrant must at least match the advertising of existing firms if it is to gain entry into the market.

▶ This increases the cost of entry and the risks of production since it represents an increase in fixed costs, that is, costs that are incurred before even a single unit is sold.

▶ Another form of non-price competition is **extended guarantees** and **warranties**. For example, by extending the period for which a product is guaranteed or by including parts and labour in the warranty, firms differentiate their product from that of rival firms.

▶ Firms might also compete by offering promotion offers such as 'two for the price of one' or 'X% extra free'. Sometimes they offer two different products so that when one is purchased the other is given 'free'.

▶ Model and style changes are another form of non-price competition. The aim is to provide a more modern (and more efficient) product than that offered by rival firms.

Contestable markets

▶ The theory of **contestable markets** implies that many of the benefits of perfect competition can be achieved as long as there are no barriers to entry or exit. It is the *threat of entry* rather than *actual entry* that is important here.

▶ The number of firms in the industry is not crucial. It is the ease of entry and exit which is important.

▶ The airline industry is sometimes suggested as a case in point. It is relatively easy for existing carriers to divert flights away from one location to take advantage of a price or cost differential in another location.

▶ When there are low entry and low exit costs, firms – even monopoly firms – will operate as if they existed in a highly competitive environment.

▶ Crucially, firms will only earn normal profit because the existence of supernormal profit would encourage new firms to enter the industry.

▶ They will also operate with maximum efficiency (i.e. lowest average cost). If this were not the case, then again lower-cost suppliers would enter the industry and undercut existing suppliers.

▶ The theory of contestable markets implies that there is no case for regulating industry in order to avoid the abuses of monopoly power. Free markets, with no barriers to entry, guarantee the benefits of competition, whether or not there are few or many firms actually in the industry.

▶ The implication is that the benefits of privatization and deregulation, by opening up markets to competition, might be considerable.

▶ In practice, the heavy fixed costs involved in actual entry to most industries implies that the number of markets which are contestable might be limited. It would be difficult for a new firm to enter chemical production or shipbuilding, for example.

▶ Again in some cases, technical expertise is required to enter an industry and this is often protected by patent rights, which limit the availability of knowledge to new firms which existing firms have gained through research and development.

▶ Existing producers are also unlikely to accept a new entrant without some form of retaliation. Existing firms might currently charge prices high enough to generate supernormal profit, but be prepared to cut prices and even run at a temporary loss if a new firm entered the industry. This action is referred to as **predatory pricing**, and although it is illegal in the UK, it is not always easy to prove that firms are behaving in this way.

Privatization

▶ An industry is privatized when equity is created and sold to investors.

▶ One problem is to determine the price at which equity is to be sold, since there may be no existing market in the assets to be offered for sale.

▶ The government has so far avoided selling equity through tender (i.e. to the highest bidder). Instead it has opted to set a price which is considered high enough to generate maximum revenue from asset sales, but low enough to ensure that the entire issue is taken up by investors.

▶ Some of the issues concerning privatization are discussed on p. 79 but one important problem is to ensure that the public utilities, some of which are arguably natural monopolies, do not abuse their newly acquired commercial freedom.

▶ To avoid this, the government has set up regulatory bodies, such as OFTEL (Office for Telecommunications), whose function it is to ensure that natural monopolies do not exploit their position to earn supernormal profits.

▶ In addition, some privatized organizations have their price changes limited by the RPI – X formula. The RPI is, of course, the retail prices index (see p. 43) and X is set by the regulatory body according to its view of what is considered a 'satisfactory' return to shareholders.

▶ Hence, if the RPI rises by 3 per cent and X is set at 1 per cent, then the price increase implied by the RPI – X formula is, $3\% - 1\% = 2\%$.

▶ The aim is to encourage efficiency, since it is only by reducing costs by *more than* X% that the newly privatized organizations can raise prices in real terms and thereby generate higher profits.

▶ The problem with this approach is that if X is increased too often, firms will lose the incentive to increase efficiency because the gains from this will be dissipated as X rises. Some of the regulatory bodies have, in fact, been criticized for increasing X by too much and too often.

Deregulation

► The aim of **deregulation** is to expose markets to competition, which is otherwise discouraged because regulations restrict the activities of firms or prevent the entry of new firms into the industry.
► It has been argued that by preventing competition, regulations have led to higher prices and lower levels of efficiency.
► Regulations were often established with the aim of protecting the public or investors, or to preserve a privileged position in some way.
► For example, competition on bus routes was prevented because of the need for bus operators to acquire a licence in order to operate a particular service. The aim was to avoid 'wasteful' duplication of services and to assist in the enforcement of safety regulations.
► Competition is now considered a more effective way of protecting the public, and, if services are duplicated by rival firms, it is argued that the public benefits from this!

REVISION ACTIVITIES

1 Explain why firms might remain in the industry in the short run even though they are making a loss.
2 A firm currently sells the same product in three completely separate markets and the following information is known:

Quantity	Market A		Market B		Market C	
	Price £	Marginal revenue £	Price £	Marginal revenue £	Price £	Marginal revenue £
1	10	22	10	24	10	18
2	9	20	9	20	9	16
3	8	18	8	16	8	14
4	7	16	7	12	7	12
5	6	14	6	8	6	10

The firm has a maximum output per period of 9 units and marginal costs for whole output of £16. How should the firm distribute its output between markets A, B and C in order to maximize profit, and what price should be charged in each market? Assume that at whatever level of output the firm produces, it at least breaks even.

PRACTICE QUESTIONS

Question 1

(a) Distinguish between the behaviour of firms in competitive and collusive oligopoly. [*12 marks*]
(b) Discuss the view that provided firms are free to enter and leave oligopolistic markets, there is no need for the government to intervene to protect the interest of consumers. [*13 marks*]

AEB

Question 2

(a) Why has the UK government followed a policy of privatization since 1979? [*15 marks*]

(b) Discuss how successful privatization has been in the United Kingdom. [*10 marks*]

WJEC

Question 3

Do you agree that any programme of privatization which merely replaces a public monopoly with a private monopoly is a failure?

London

3 Market failure

- ▶ Allocative inefficiency
- ▶ Deadweight loss
- ▶ Externality
- ▶ Free rider
- ▶ Merit goods

- ▶ Private cost
- ▶ Property rights
- ▶ Public goods
- ▶ Social benefit
- ▶ Social cost

✓ REVISION TIPS

In recent years, economic policy in countries the world over has emphasized the importance of freeing markets from regulation and reigning back the frontiers of state involvement in the economy. There is little doubt that free markets are very much in favour at the moment, but this does not imply that markets always discharge their role efficiently. The increasing emphasis on the role of markets has been accompanied by a growth of interest in the notion of **market failure**. You must therefore be fully aware of what market failure implies, why it arises and the different ways in which it might be corrected. In particular, be aware of the relative advantages that some correction strategies have over other strategies, and ensure you are able to discuss these in detail!

◉ TOPIC OUTLINE

- ▶ Markets allocate resources optimally when the price consumers pay for the last unit of a good they consume exactly equals the cost of attracting resources away from the next most desired alternative. In other words, the price consumers pay for the last unit of a good they consume exactly equals its **marginal cost** of production – that is, the cost of producing one more unit (see pp. 31–32).
- ▶ Market failure implies that the free operation of the **price mechanism** fails to allocate resources optimally. In this sense, the market allocates resources inefficiently because the price of the last unit consumed is not equated with its marginal cost of production or because some other 'distortion' occurs.
- ▶ Market failure can sometimes be corrected without government intervention. However, the existence of market failure provides a powerful reason for government intervention in the economy.
- ▶ To understand how market failure can be corrected it is *essential* to understand the **causes** of market failure.

Externalities

- ▶ An **externality** is created when some activity of an economic agent (individual, firm or government) affects the wellbeing of another economic agent.
- ▶ Externalities are common in acts of production and consumption, and they confer either positive effects or negative effects on those members of society affected by them.

► An example of a **negative externality** occurs when a factory belches smoke into the environment so that the neighbourhood around the factory loses its access to clean air. The firm benefits because it has access to a relatively cheap method of disposing of its smoke, but society loses its access to clean air. In other words, part of the cost of smoke disposal is borne by society generally, rather than the actual polluter, which disposes of its waste **free of charge**.

► An example of a **positive externality** occurs when an individual is vaccinated against a contagious disease. The individual benefits because that person cannot contract the disease, and society also benefits because there is a reduced risk of the disease being passed on to other members of society. In other words, part of the benefit of an individual being vaccinated against a contagious disease is passed on to other members of society **free of charge**.

► Externalities therefore involve a cost or a benefit that is not reflected in the price of the product but which is passed on to society generally, rather than to the economic agent generating the externality.

► These external costs and benefits are important in assessing the allocation of resources and in enabling economists to consider the full **social costs** and **social benefits** of production.

► The **social cost** of production is the private or internal cost (i.e. the cost of resources such as labour, electricity, raw materials and so on) plus the external costs (i.e. the money value of any negative externalities).

► The **social benefit** of consumption is the private or internal benefit (i.e. the private benefits, or personal satisfaction, from consumption) plus the external benefit of consumption (i.e. the money value of any positive externalities).

Allocative efficiency with externalities

► It is important to know the way in which externalities affect output decisions and result in **allocative inefficiency** or **market failure**.

► In Figure 3.1, $S_0 S_0$ and $D_0 D_0$ are the supply and demand conditions that exist in production and consumption when there are *no* externalities. These conditions are true for many products. For example, my consumption of an apple is unlikely to confer any social benefit on someone else! Similarly, if I am a grower of flowers, this is unlikely to impose any external cost on other members of society. In these cases, social cost and social benefit are equal to private cost and private benefit.

► When this equality occurs, resources are allocated optimally, at least in a competitive market (see Chapter 2), because the price consumers pay for the

Figure 3.1 Free markets allocate resources optimally when private and social marginal benefit are equal and private and social marginal cost are equal. In this case, P_0 and Q_0 are the equilibrium and socially efficient price and quantity. If, instead, S_0 reflects only private costs and S_s is the full social cost supply curve, free markets will allocate resources suboptimally and the appropriate price and quantity should be P_1 and Q_1

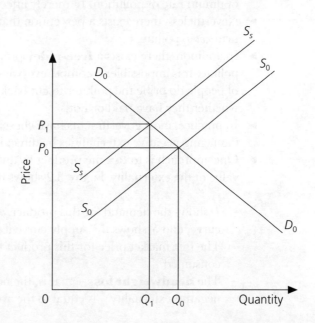

last unit they consume exactly equals its full **marginal social cost of production**.

▶ In this case, resources are allocated optimally when the price is P_0 and Q_0 units are produced and consumed.

▶ However, suppose production is undertaken by a firm dumping toxic waste into a river? In this instance, private cost and social cost diverge. The curve S_sS_s is the supply curve for the product, based on both the private and social cost of production.

▶ Hence, when P_0 and Q_0 are the equilibrium price and quantity, resources are *not* allocated optimally. The price consumers pay for the last unit they consume does not reflect its full marginal social cost of production.

▶ Society is overconsuming this product and, therefore, resources are not allocated optimally because if price reflected the full marginal social cost of production, society would choose to consume less of this product and resources would then be diverted to other products which society values more highly.

▶ An optimal allocation of resources requires that price is P_1 and Q_1 units are produced and consumed. In other words, Q_0Q_1 resources are diverted to other uses.

▶ However, few if any firms will ever voluntarily produce where price equals the full **marginal social cost of production**, because they would be deliberately reducing their profitability. In our case, if the firm constructed a chamber so that smoke was not emitted into the atmosphere, it would raise its private costs of production. In other words, it would **internalize** the externality and, by so doing, would reduce its profits from production.

▶ Failure voluntarily to reduce the externality provides a reason for government intervention, either to restrict the ability of the polluter to pollute or to make the polluter pay for the pollution caused.

▶ The **Coase theorem** offers one approach to pollution control and suggests the establishment of **property rights**. Thus, if a law is passed which entitles those in the neighbourhood of the factory to breathe clean air and the right to sue if not, then it may be logical for a polluter to compensate households for the pollution generated. Alternatively, if a polluter is given the right to pollute in law, then it may be logical for those affected by pollution to bribe the polluter not to pollute. In both cases there may be scope for pollution to be restricted to the socially optimum level (MSB = MSC).

▶ This is an important point because it implies that no matter who pays – the victim or the polluter – the outcome is the same: pollution can be restricted to the optimum level.

▶ The suggestion is that who compensates whom is irrelevant to achieving the optimum rate of pollution. It merely affects the distribution of income.

▶ Nevertheless, there exists a perception that it would be unfair for society to pay a firm *not* to pollute.

▶ In addition, there exists a **free-rider** problem with bribing polluters not to pollute. It is impossible to compel everyone to pay, and yet, if a sufficient number of people do bribe the polluter to cut back, all households in the vicinity benefit whether they have paid or not!

▶ In practice, most governments have chosen to deal with the most obvious and damaging negative externalities by direct intervention.

▶ One approach is to **tax** the product by an amount per unit equal to the marginal value of the externality. Figure 3.2 shows how this solution would work:

  – D shows the demand for this product, while S_f shows the free market supply curve, and S_s shows the supply curve if social costs are taken into consideration.
  – The free market price for this product is, P_f and, at this price, Q_f units are consumed.
  – The **deadweight loss** – that is, the net welfare loss to society caused by the negative externality – is equal to the area ABC. This is the loss of consumer

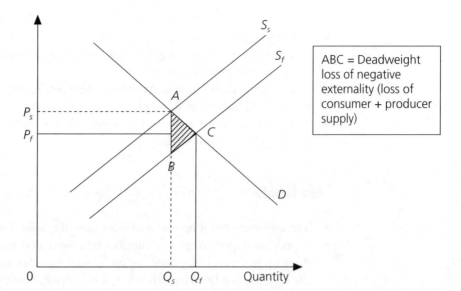

Figure 3.2 Using a tax to eliminate the deadweight loss of a negative externality such as pollution

ABC = Deadweight loss of negative externality (loss of consumer + producer supply)

surplus and producer surplus when we compare the free market equilibrium (*C*) with the social optimum equilibrium (*A*).

– If a tax is imposed on this product equal to AB per unit, the price of the product would rise to P_s and consumption would fall to Q_s. The deadweight loss would disappear and the tax would therefore ensure that production was at the optimum rate.

In this way, taxing the polluter achieves the optimal level of pollution.

▶ A different approach to pollution control is to create **pollution permits** that give the right to pollute up to a specified amount. Any firm polluting above this level is taxed on the amount of pollution it generates. This approach is discussed in the answer to Question 3 (see pp. 104–105).

Public goods and merit goods

▶ A different kind of market failure arises when under a market system, only those products which can be sold at a profit are produced.
▶ Some products, such as national defence and street lighting, possess special characteristics which prevent them from being supplied through the market.
▶ By their very nature, such products are **non-excludable** and **non-rival**.
▶ They are **non-excludable** because if they are provided for one person it is impossible to prevent others (non-payers) from consuming them. For example, it is impossible to provide street lighting for one person but prevent others from consuming it. This is referred to as the **free-rider** problem. It is, therefore, difficult to enforce a price for such products.
▶ They are **non-rival** because consumption by one person does not diminish the amount available for consumption by others. For example, my consumption of national defence does not reduce the amount available for others. The true marginal cost of provision is arguably zero, implying a zero price for an optimum resource allocation.
▶ Goods which possess these twin characteristics are referred to as **public goods**.
▶ Because no one would ever pay individually for these goods or services, the market would fail to supply them. Hence, if they are to be provided at all, they must be provided free at the point of consumption by the state.
▶ **Merit goods** are different from public goods because they are neither non-excludable nor non-rival. They *could* therefore be provided through the market.
▶ However, merit goods confer positive externalities on society and therefore would be **underconsumed** if they were provided through the market.

- The most often quoted examples of merit goods are education and health care.
- Both these goods confer positive externalities on society because a healthier, better-educated society is a more productive society, and the more society produces, the more it can consume.
- If these goods were provided through the market, only those willing and able to pay would have access to them.
- To ensure that there is no underconsumption of these merit goods, they are provided freely through the state.

Monopoly

- The existence of monopoly is also a cause of market failure.
- A pure monopoly is the sole supplier of a particular product and has the power to drive up price and so reduce consumption below the optimum level. This is still the case when a broader definition of monopoly is adopted, i.e. more than one quarter of output in the hands of a single firm or group of linked firms.
- An optimal allocation of resources exists when the price consumers pay for the last unit they consume *exactly equals* its marginal cost of production. Under *perfect competition* the **MC curve** of the firm and industry is the **supply curve** of the firm and industry. In Figure 3.3 below this would give price P_1 and quantity Q_1 in equilibrium, with price exactly equal to *MC*.
- The price consumers pay for the last unit they consume measures their assessment of the value of the last unit in comparison with alternatives.
- Marginal cost is the additional cost the firm incurs when one more unit is produced: that is, it is the cost of attracting resources away from alternatives.
- When the price consumers pay for the last unit they consume *exactly equals* its marginal cost of production, the value consumers place on the last unit of the product they consume exactly equals its opportunity cost of production.
- The inefficiency loss to society of monopoly is measured by the area *ABC* in Figure 3.3. Under 'pure' monopoly the demand curve for the industry (*D*) is now the demand and average revenue curve for the firm.
- In Figure 3.3, the profit-maximising price (*MC* = *MR*) of the product is *P*, and *Q* units are supplied and demanded. However, at this price and output combination, price *exceeds* marginal cost, and this is the case until output is expanded to Q_1 and price has fallen to P_1.
- This implies that the area *ABC* is **deadweight loss**: that is, it is the welfare loss to society from the activities of the monopolist. It corresponds to the loss of

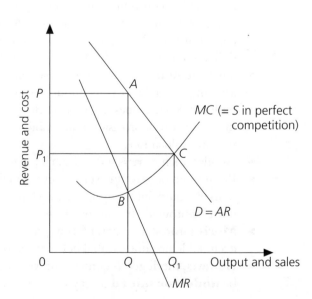

Figure 3.3   Deadweight loss under monopoly

consumer surplus and producer surplus when comparing the outcome at Q_1 with that at Q.

▶ Note that the above argument rests on the assumption that the marginal private cost of production (i.e. MC in Figure 3.3) is the same as the **marginal social cost of production**.

★ REVISION ACTIVITIES

1 With the aid of an appropriate diagram, show why, if individuals had to pay to be vaccinated against a contagious disease such as smallpox, consumption of vaccinations would be less than the optimal level.

2 In what circumstances can the allocation of resources be improved by an **increase** in the level of pollution?

3 How might free state provision of merit goods such as health care lead to a misallocation of resources?

PRACTICE QUESTIONS

Question 1

'Road congestion is a result of market failure.'

(a) Explain the meaning of the above statement. [*30 marks*]

(b) Examine the policies which a government might pursue to deal with the problem of road congestion. [*70 marks*]

London

Question 2

(a) Explain why environmental pollution is regarded as a source of market failure. [*12 marks*]

(b) Evaluate *two* different policies which a government might implement to reduce pollution. [*13 marks*]

AEB

Question 3

(a) Explain and illustrate what is meant by the term 'externalities'. [*10 marks*]

(b) If a good or service gives rise to an externality, should it be provided by the government? [*15 marks*]

UCLES

4 Inequality and poverty

KEY CONCEPTS

- ▶ Gini coefficient
- ▶ Income
- ▶ Lorenz curve

- ▶ Minimum wage
- ▶ Negative income tax
- ▶ Wealth

REVISION TIPS

It is important to be clear about the distinction between income and wealth. Income is a **flow** of funds received over time. Wealth is the accumulated value of assets and is therefore regarded as a **stock**.

The distribution of income and wealth is an emotive issue and it is sometimes tempting to analyse these from a particular political stance. Of course, you are entitled to an opinion on what you consider to be the most appropriate distribution of income and wealth, but take care not to let your opinion cloud your judgement when analysing the facts.

Questions on inequality of income often ask why one group of workers receives more than another group. Be sure that you can explain the existence of pay differentials. The adoption of a national minimum wage is also topical at the moment and you should be clear about the implications of this.

TOPIC OUTLINE

Measuring inequality

- ▶ The most common measure of the distribution of income is the **Lorenz curve**. This shows the **percentage** of income earned by households at successive levels of income. A typical Lorenz curve is illustrated in Figure 4.1

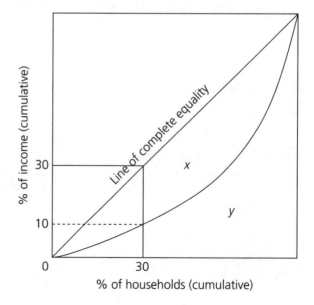

Figure 4.1 A Lorenz curve shows the distribution of income within an economy

▶ The 45° line or diagonal in Figure 4.1 is simply for comparison since it shows the situation that would exist if there was *absolute equality* in the distribution of income. For example, 30% of households would receive 30% of income.

▶ The more *bowed* the Lorenz curve, the greater the inequality in the distribution of income. For example, 30% of households receive only 10% of income in Figure 4.1.

▶ The **Gini coefficient** (G) is sometimes used to assess the extent of inequality. To compute this, simply divide the area between the 45° line and the Lorenz curve by the area under the 45° line: that is, divide area x by area $x + y$. For *perfect equality*, G = 0; for *perfect inequality*, G = 1. The closer to 0 the value of G is, the more equality exists.

Sources of inequality in the distribution of income

Much of the following discussion could be related to simple demand/supply analysis in the *labour market* (Figure 4.2). Anything which tends to shift the supply curve to the left for a particular occupation, or the demand curve to the right, will tend to *raise* wages and vice versa. Do remember that the demand for any factor is derived from the demand for the good or service it produces.

Differences in ability

▶ People have different mental and physical abilities and this limits the choice of occupation available to certain individuals. Not everyone has the mental ability to become a barrister and not everyone has the physical ability to become a professional athlete! At the other end of the spectrum, many people have the mental ability to become an office clerk or the physical ability to become an unskilled worker. Restrictions of supply tend to raise wages, surpluses of supply to lower wages, other things being equal.

Discrimination

▶ At the workplace, discrimination occurs when workers are treated differently (or are denied access to certain occupations) on the basis of race or gender etc. Any restriction of supply via discrimination can raise the wages of those discriminating. However those discriminated against may be forced into a limited number of less attractive occupations, thereby increasing supply and lowering wages.

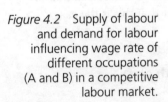

Figure 4.2 Supply of labour and demand for labour influencing wage rate of different occupations (A and B) in a competitive labour market.

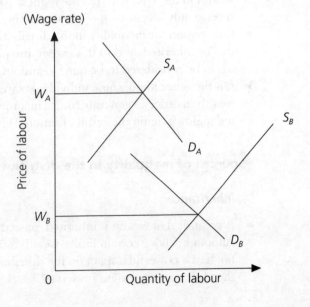

Occupational differences

▶ Given a choice, most people would prefer to work in a clean, pleasant, non-dangerous environment. In other words, some occupations offer a higher degree of utility to workers than others. Most people would agree, for example, that a teacher works in a better environment than a coal miner.

▶ Because of this factor, **compensating wage differentials** exist in some occupations, and, *to the extent that they do*, inequality in wages might be said to be partly the result of choice. A less attractive occupation may provide higher wages than a more attractive occupation, *without* bringing about movements between the occupations (i.e. supply) to remove the differential.

▶ Similarly, some people place a higher value on leisure than on income, and so *choose* to work fewer hours than others (for example, in part-time employment).

Human capital investment choices

▶ Some people choose to undertake training or stay in education beyond the minimum school-leaving age rather than go directly into employment. Just as firms invest in plant and equipment to increase future profits, so some individuals invest in themselves to increase future earnings.

▶ Investment in human capital (as economists refer to education and training) increases productivity and, therefore, the likelihood of higher lifetime earnings.

▶ If all other things are equal, this view implies that some of the observed earnings inequality is the result of rational choices on the part of individuals. Some of the extra earnings of individuals being a return on their extra investment in human capital.

Random factors

▶ There is no doubt that random factors influence the earnings of certain individuals. Technological change can result in a fall in demand for certain skills and, in such cases, the earnings of individuals who possess those skills are almost certain to fall. Soccer stars, for instance, might sustain an injury which terminates their career prematurely.

Possession of wealth

▶ Some individuals derive considerable income from their assets, such as property, bonds and equity.

▶ The distribution of wealth is more uneven than the distribution of income. For example, the most wealthy 25 per cent owns over 70 per cent of total marketable wealth in the UK, whereas the highest 20 per cent of income earners in the UK receive only 38 per cent of net disposable income.

▶ One reason for inequality in the distribution of wealth is, of course, that wealth can be inherited, and to this extent, inequality in the distribution of income might again be considered to be due to random factors.

▶ On the other hand, some individuals save out of current income to accumulate wealth in order to generate future income. To the extent that this is the case, inequality is again the result of rational choice.

Sources of inequality in the distribution of wealth

Inheritance

▶ A great deal of wealth is inherited, passed on from one generation to the next. Although, above certain limits, wealth is taxed when it is transferred, taxation has not had a powerful impact on the distribution of wealth. Existing inequalities are therefore to some extent preserved.

Wealth creates wealth

► Owners of wealth derive incomes from their wealth which can then be used to acquire additional assets, thus adding to wealth. Those with little wealth usually spend most of their income on consumption.

The effect of inflation

► *Inflation* often benefits holders of wealth since many assets rise in value by more than the rate of inflation and so provide a useful store of value. This is particularly true of land and property. Wealthier individuals therefore benefit from inflation to a greater extent than those with fewer assets.

Random factors

► Some inequality in the distribution of wealth is the result of random factors. Jackpot winners on the National Lottery, for example, no doubt invest part of their windfall gain in assets.

The effects of income inequality

► The price mechanism works in the labour market as well as in the product market. Changes in the demand for different products lead to changes in the derived demand for different types of labour which produce these products.
► This, in turn, leads to changes in wage rates offered in different occupations and so to a reallocation of labour away from declining sectors and into expanding sectors.
► Differences in earnings may encourage individuals to invest in human capital. Without such differentials, fewer people would spend time training or remain in education beyond the legal minimum. This would have serious implications for future economic growth (see Chapter 7).
► Differences in income also provide a spur to effort and initiative. After all, the quest for higher earnings is the main reason most people seek promotion.
► On the other hand, income inequality gives the wealthier members of society greater influence over the range of goods and services produced than is the case for those on lower incomes. Remember, the price mechanism conveys the **effective demands** of society, not simply the **desires**.
► Inequality also leads to **poverty**, difficult though it is to define. Poverty can lead to deprivation, alienation, crime and other undesirable conditions. All governments take action to reduce the impact of poverty which implies that society considers it an undesirable effect of income inequality.

Poverty

► The causes of **poverty** are the same as the causes of inequality. Poverty exists because of differences in human skills and abilities, limited investment in human capital, and so on.
► The problem is to define exactly what is meant by poverty. It is easy to observe inequality. Poverty, however, is a relative term and is not so easily defined.
► Poverty is sometimes defined as a situation that exists when an individual or family has an income below some minimum level. This is referred to as the **absolute poverty standard**.
► A different approach is based on the recognition that whether a person considers themselves to be poor depends on the lifestyles of other people around them. A **relative poverty standard** defines the poor as having an income below, say, 30 per cent of the average household income.

Measures to reduce inequality

▶ The most obvious method of reducing inequality is through the **tax system**.

▶ In the UK, income tax is **progressive** (i.e. the marginal rate of tax exceeds the average rate of tax), so that the higher income earners pay **proportionately** more of their income in taxation than lower income earners.

▶ Similarly, VAT is *not* levied on certain goods that account for a higher proportion of expenditure for lower income groups than for higher income groups (e.g. foodstuffs).

▶ The **state** also makes certain goods and services freely available. In the UK, education has been freely available from school to university. Health care has also been freely available through the National Health Service.

▶ The **benefit system** also helps relieve poverty. Social security benefits give those on incomes below a certain level a cash payment.

▶ Some goods are **subsidized** by the state. However, subsidies are indiscriminate and benefit *all* consumers, not just those on low incomes.

Minimum wages

▶ The adoption of a **minimum wage** is very much a controversial issue, although some sort of minimum wage currently exists in most industrialized countries.

▶ The case for the adoption of a minimum wage is largely based on grounds of equity. It is a means of ensuring that the earnings of workers do not fall below some minimum level. Evidence suggests that some occupations, such as catering and the production of clothing, are traditionally low paid. A national minimum wage would terminate this situation. There is also the argument that low wage firms rely on the state to top-up the earnings of their employees with income support and other state benefits. Low wages therefore contribute to a growing welfare state, requiring high taxes etc. to finance it.

▶ In the UK, the implementation of a minimum wage has been resisted for several reasons.

▶ One view held by many is that markets operate most efficiently when they are free of government interference. This is arguably true of the labour market as much as any other market.

▶ It is also considered that by limiting the extent to which wages can fall, the adoption of a minimum wage will reduce the ability of the labour market to reallocate labour in response to changes in supply and demand conditions.

▶ A further argument is that the adoption of a minimum wage would lead to unemployment. By increasing wage rates *above* the equilibrium level in some labour markets, it is argued that a minimum wage would lead to an excess supply of labour in these markets and hence unemployment.

▶ Whether this happens depends on the extent to which increased labour costs can be passed on by firms in the form of higher prices, and this, in turn, depends on the price elasticity of demand for their products.

▶ Thus, to the extent that labour costs rise, a minimum wage might stimulate cost-push inflation in the economy.

▶ As a result of rising costs, firms would find it more difficult to compete in export markets, while imports would become more competitive in the domestic market. This implies an adverse effect on the current account of the balance of payments.

▶ Another way in which the adoption of a minimum wage might increase unemployment is if it discourages firms from taking on workers, particularly the young and unskilled, who might now be regarded as 'too expensive' given their limited contribution to firm output.

▶ If fewer young workers are taken on, less training might be undertaken, thus creating a skill shortage in the future which will reduce the potential for economic growth.

▶ On the other hand, if the adoption of a minimum wage encourages firms to substitute capital for labour, this might have a beneficial effect on future economic growth.

▶ The minimum wage is a complex issue. Try to use *economic analysis*, including simple supply and demand diagrams of the labour market, to answer questions.

A negative income tax

▶ A different solution to the problem of low pay is a **negative income tax**. The basic idea is to establish a **minimum income guarantee** which is fixed in cash terms according to the circumstances (number of dependants, etc.) of each particular family.

▶ This minimum income guarantee is paid in full to those without any other form of income. Thereafter the whole of a person's earned income is taxed at the appropriate rate.

▶ For example, suppose the minimum income guarantee is £3,000 and earned income is taxed at the rate of 30 per cent. When a family has no other income, it receives the full minimum income guarantee. When household income rises – for example, because someone in the household obtains employment – each additional pound earned reduces benefit paid by the state by £0.30p.

▶ When household income rises to £10,000, the minimum income guarantee is withdrawn (i.e. 30 per cent × £10,000 = £3,000) and thereafter tax is paid to the state rather than benefit received from the state.

▶ One advantage of this proposal is that it would remove the effect of the **unemployment** and **poverty traps**. Because of the current way in which tax is levied on earned income and benefit is withdrawn, many people are discouraged from seeking employment because they are financially worse off in employment than when they are unemployed! Effectively they are facing marginal tax rates from moving into employment close to, or even above 100%; this is called the 'unemployment trap'.

▶ A negative income tax would ensure that people were *always* better off in employment than unemployed. It might therefore have a powerful impact on the numbers employed!

REVISION ACTIVITIES

1 Does the fact that, on average, women earn about two-thirds the earnings of men prove conclusively that sex discrimination exists?
2 Education is more equally distributed than earnings. Why is this?
3 If, over time, the Gini coefficient was decreasing, what does this imply about how the distribution of income is changing?

PRACTICE QUESTIONS

Question 1
'Trade unions can only increase their members' wages if they are prepared to accept job losses.' Discuss

WJEC

Question 2
(a) Explain why the average salary of a secretary is less than the average salary of a solicitor. [*12 marks*]

(b) Discuss the importance of wage differentials for the efficient functioning of a market economy. [*13 marks*]

AEB

Question 3

Discuss the advantages and disadvantages of the following policies as methods for reducing poverty:

(a) Increasing social security benefits such as unemployment benefit (Job Seekers' Allowance), child benefit and state pensions; [*9 marks*]
(b) reductions in income tax; [*8 marks*]
(c) subsidies for food, fuel and housing. [*8 marks*]

WJEC

5 Inflation and unemployment

KEY CONCEPTS

- ► Aggregate demand
- ► Aggregate supply
- ► Balance of payments
- ► Consumption
- ► Current account
- ► Equation of exchange
- ► Exports
- ► Government expenditure
- ► Imports
- ► Inflation

- ► Investment
- ► Natural rate of output
- ► Natural rate of unemployment
- ► Phillips curve
- ► Price level
- ► Quantity theory of money
- ► Real balance effect
- ► Retail prices index
- ► Supply-side economics
- ► Unemployment

REVISION TIPS

Inflation and **unemployment** are core topics in any course on macroeconomic theory and policy and A-level Economics is certainly no exception. Inflation, especially when it is variable and unpredictable, has far-reaching consequences and, despite any short-run gains, it is always ultimately destructive in its effects. For this reason, inflation is usually regarded by economists as public enemy number one. However, a dilemma exists for policy-makers because, in some circumstances, the short-run gains from higher inflation might last long enough, and be significant enough, to encourage them to generate inflation – despite the long-run costs! It is therefore important that you fully understand the nature of the trade-off between inflation and unemployment in both the short run and the long run. You must also be familiar with the gains that might come initially with inflation and the costs that it ultimately imposes.

Take care not to confuse changes in the **price level** with changes in the **rate of inflation**. The price level simply refers to the average of all final prices. A change in the price level implies a one-off movement from one price level to another price level. A change in the rate of inflation implies that the price level is changing at a different rate. For example, a rise in the annual rate of inflation from 2 per cent to 3 per cent implies that the price level is now rising by 3 per cent per year instead of its previous rate of 2 per cent per year.

Economic policy in the 1990s is largely directed towards controlling inflation and improving efficiency through **supply-side policies**. Be aware of the supply side policies that have been introduced in recent years in the UK economy (or your own economy if this is different), and the impact of such policies on output and employment.

TOPIC OUTLINE

- ► In broad terms, the **rate of inflation** provides an indication of the rate at which the average price level is rising, and the **level of unemployment** provides an indication of the extent of idle resources in the economy.
- ► The main official measure of the rate of inflation in the UK is the **retail prices index (RPI)**. A rise in the RPI is interpreted as a rise in the rate of inflation and

a fall in the RPI as a fall in the rate of inflation. A fall in the RPI does not imply that the average level of prices is falling (unless the change in the RPI is negative). Instead, it implies that, on average, prices are rising *more slowly* than previously.

▶ In the UK, the **rate of unemployment** expresses the number who register themselves unemployed as a percentage of the labour force.

The quantity theory of money

▶ Economists have been interested in rising prices for centuries and the oldest theory in economics is the **quantity theory of money**, which, in its extreme form, predicts a proportionate relationship between changes in the quantity of money and changes in the average price level.

▶ The quantity theory of money is derived from the **equation of exchange**, which is sometimes written as:

$$MV = PY,$$

where:

M = some measure of the money supply;
V = the income velocity of circulation (i.e. the average number of times each unit of currency is used to purchase final output);
P = the average price of final output; and
Y = the volume of final output.

▶ As it stands, this equation is simply an *identity* because both sides of the equation are simply different ways of expressing the same aggregate. It must always be true that total spending (MV) is identically equal to the value of output purchased (PY).

▶ However, it is believed by many economists that **velocity** (V) is relatively stable and, for simplicity, can be treated as a **constant**. It is also now widely believed that output tends towards a **natural rate** and that this can be regarded as the long-run equilibrium rate of output. In the long run, Y can therefore also be treated as a constant. This implies that changes in the money supply (M) lead to proportional changes in the price level (P) and, in particular, that an acceleration of money growth leads to an acceleration in the rate of inflation.

▶ Velocity of circulation (V) is thought to be stable because it is determined by institutional factors such as the frequency with which wages and salaries are paid, technology (e.g. the availability of cash-point facilities), deregulation of the banking sector, and so on. Since these factors change slowly over time, velocity will change slowly over time.

▶ To explain the existence of a natural rate of output (Y) requires us to distinguish between aggregate supply in the short run and aggregate supply in the long run, and to do this we need to use the aggregate demand/aggregate supply framework.

Aggregate demand and aggregate supply

▶ **Aggregate demand** consists of total spending on domestic output. Algebraically it can be expressed as:

$$AD = C + I + G + X - M$$

where:

AD = aggregate demand;
C = consumption expenditures by households;
I = investment expenditures by firms;
G = government spending on goods and services (direct government expenditure);
X = exports (sales of output to overseas residents); and
M = imports (purchases of overseas output by domestic residents).

- ▶ Aggregate demand varies *inversely* with the price level because:
  - – As the price level *falls*, there is a **real balance effect**. In other words, the purchasing power of nominal money balances rises and this will persuade economic agents to *increase* their expenditures, and vice versa.
  - – As the price level *falls*, the rate of interest will tend to fall and this will encourage firms to *increase* their investment expenditures and vice versa.
  - – As the domestic price level *falls*, exports will become more competitive on world markets and imports will become less competitive on the domestic market. As exports rise and imports fall, aggregate demand will *increase*.
- ▶ In the short run, aggregate supply varies directly with the price level because firms undertake production on the basis of some *expected price*. Costs are incurred in anticipation of sales at this expected price. If the *actual price* at which output sells is greater than the expected price, firms will make higher profits than expected and will therefore expand production. So a rise in price will increase aggregate supply, and vice versa, in the short run.
- ▶ In the long run, however, there is a **natural rate of output** and the long-run aggregate supply curve is vertical at the natural rate of output. This implies that, in the long run, the level of output is *constant* at the natural rate irrespective of what happens to the price level.
- ▶ To see why the natural rate of output is the long-run equilibrium rate of output, consider Figure 5.1, where AD is the original aggregate demand curve, AS_S is the original short-run aggregate supply curve, and AS_L is the long-run aggregate supply curve. The economy is initially in equilibrium, with the price level at P and output at the natural rate Y.

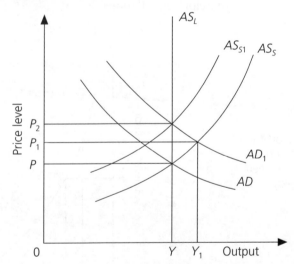

Figure 5.1 The effect of an increase in aggregate demand on output and the price level, in both the short run and the long run

- ▶ Now assume that the government *unexpectedly* increases its spending on education, and all other things remain equal. The aggregate demand curve will shift upwards to AD_1, the price level will rise to P_1 and output will rise to Y_1 as the economy moves up the short-run aggregate supply curve.
- ▶ Because the increase in government spending was unexpected, the rise in the price level is unexpected. Because costs – especially wages and salaries – are negotiated in the expectation that P would be the price level, firms have made windfall profits, but the real wages of the labour force have fallen.
- ▶ When contracts are renegotiated, trade unions will seek to raise the real wages of their members, at least to the level that existed before the rise in the price level.
- ▶ As nominal wage rates rise (to restore the real wage), the cost of producing any given level of output will rise, and so the short-run aggregate supply curve will shift upwards to AS_{S1}.
- ▶ Final equilibrium is restored when the price level has risen to P_2 and output has returned to the natural rate Y.

► The implications of the existence of a *natural rate of output* for the traditional quantity theory of money are clear. **Changes in the money supply have no impact on real output or on employment in the long run!**

► If it can be established that velocity is also unrelated to changes in the quantity of money, then the quantity theory is correct: there *is* a proportionate relationship between changes in the money supply and changes in the price level and, by implication, changes in money growth lead to changes in the rate of inflation.

The Phillips curve

► We have seen that in the short run an increase in aggregate demand leads to an increase in aggregate supply but in the long run, as aggregate supply returns to the natural rate, it leads only to an increase in the price level.

► The **Phillips curve** analyses the implications of this for the labour market. The Phillips curve hypothesizes a short-run trade-off between the rate of inflation and the rate of unemployment. A typical short-run Phillips curve is shown in Figure 5.2, which indicates an *inverse* relationship between the rate of inflation and the rate of unemployment.

► There are many possible reasons for this inverse relationship, but it seems reasonable to argue that as demand for output rises, so prices will rise and firms will recruit more staff (unemployment falls). In order to attract more workers as labour shortages develop, firms will bid up the wage rate, further stimulating inflation. However, at lower levels of aggregate demand, there will be no upward pressure on prices and, since unemployment will be greater, firms will have no difficulty recruiting and retaining staff, resulting in less pressure on wages, and therefore on inflation.

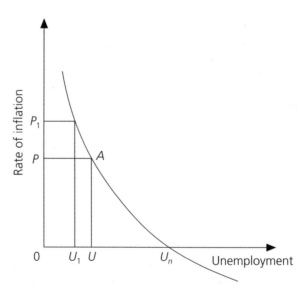

Figure 5.2 A typical short-run Phillips curve, offering policy-makers a trade-off between inflation and unemployment

► The short-run Phillips curve offers policy-makers a **menu** of policy choice. For example, the economy might be located at point A on the Phillips curve. However, if policy-makers wish to reduce unemployment below its current rate of U to a lower level U_1, they must accept a higher rate of inflation P_1 instead of P.

► In Figure 5.2, U_n is the **natural rate of unemployment**. To see why, consider Figure 5.3 which shows the same Phillips curve, this time labelled $P^{e=0}$ to imply that the expected rate of inflation is zero. Now assume that the authorities increase the money supply by 2 per cent. The implied increase in aggregate demand will generate higher prices, and real profits will increase because input costs are initially fixed so that higher prices imply higher profits.

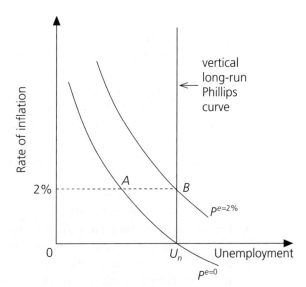

Figure 5.3 The short-run and the long-run Phillips curve

- ▶ Higher real profits will encourage firms to increase output and, in order to attract more workers, they will increase nominal wage rates. The economy moves up the short-run Phillips curve from U_n to point A.
- ▶ However, this is not a permanent equilibrium position. When wage rates are renegotiated, workers will demand compensation to restore their real wages to the levels that existed before the rise in prices. Once real wages are restored to their previous levels, real profits will also be at their previous levels because wages and prices will both have increased by the same amount, in this case by 2 per cent.
- ▶ The previous incentive for firms to increase output and employment has therefore disappeared, and output and employment/unemployment will therefore both return to the natural rate.
- ▶ It is important to note that prices are now 2 per cent higher and the expected rate of inflation is now 2 per cent. A new short-run Phillips curve exists because, although the economy moves up the short run Phillips curve $P^{e=0}$ it does *not* move down the same Phillips curve.
- ▶ The economy moves instead to point B and the appropriate short-run Phillips curve is now $P^{e=2\%}$ because the actual and expected rate of inflation is now 2 per cent. If there should be any further, unanticipated increases in the money supply, the economy will move up to this new curve $P^{e=2\%}$.
- ▶ In the long run, the Phillips curve is vertical at the natural rate of unemployment U_n and this is the rate of unemployment that exists when output is at the natural rate, Y in Figure 5.1.
- ▶ Whether we consider Figure 5.1 or Figure 5.3, it seems that there is an exploitable short-run trade-off between inflation and output/employment.
- ▶ However, the authorities might not choose to exploit this short-run trade-off because the short-run gains might be so temporary as to be outweighed by the cost of higher long-run inflation.
- ▶ Before we consider the problems generated by a higher rate of inflation, it is worth considering why the existence of a short-run trade-off might not encourage governments to accept higher inflation in return for (temporarily) higher output and employment.
- ▶ The answer to this question is that the gains from increased output and employment are very short-lived. Indeed, they may even be non-existent, when the effects of an expansionary monetary policy are perfectly anticipated by economic agents.
- ▶ When economic agents form their expectations rationally, they consider all relevant information in assessing the future value of a particular variable.
- ▶ For example, if economic agents know from past history that an expansion of the money supply leads, in the long run, only to an increase in the price level, with no

lasting impact on output and employment, then prices and wages will be adjusted more quickly than otherwise.

▶ The more quickly wages and prices are adjusted, the shorter is the adjustment period to reach long-run equilibrium.

▶ Indeed if there is perfect flexibility of wages and prices, there will be no short-run gains in output and employment. Following an increase in the money supply, the economy will simply move from one long-run equilibrium position to a new long-run equilibrium position, at which nominal wages and prices will be higher, but the real wage and real price level will be the same as before the increase in the money supply!

▶ If an increase in money growth simply leads to a higher rate of inflation, what is the problem? Why do governments worry about the rate of inflation?

▶ In fact, the main problem with inflation, especially when it is variable and unpredictable, is that it leads to inefficiencies in the allocation of resources.

▶ It does this because it prevents the price mechanism from giving **accurate information** to producers and consumers about changes in society's tastes.

▶ To see why, consider a retailer who notices a rise in price for a particular product. The retailer will interpret this as a change in society's preferences such that society now demands more of this particular product. The retailer will therefore order more of this particular product and producers will produce more. Resources will therefore be competed away from alternatives. This is how the price mechanism allocates resources.

▶ However, what if the rise in price observed by the retailer did not reflect a change in society's preferences at all? What if it was simply the first sign of a general rise in prices as part of the inflationary process?

▶ How can the retailer tell the difference? In fact, it is impossible to do so, and so the implication is clear. Inflation *distorts* the price signals transmitted by the price mechanism and so impairs the efficiency with which the price mechanism allocates resources.

▶ There are, of course, other problems with inflation that make it undesirable. One problem is that inflation arbitrarily redistributes income from lenders to borrowers. It does this because the purchasing power of any amount lent is reduced by inflation when repayment is made.

▶ It might be possible, however, for lenders to protect themselves from this by ensuring that the nominal rate of interest is above the rate of inflation. Nevertheless, to the extent that lenders are unable to do this, real income will be redistributed in favour of borrowers.

▶ Inflation also redistributes income from those on fixed incomes, such as pensioners, in favour of those whose incomes are in some way linked to inflation, such as those who are self-employed.

▶ Another problem with inflation is that when it is above the rate experienced in other countries, it reduces the competitiveness of exports on international markets and increases the competitiveness of imports on the domestic market. The result is likely to be a deficit on the current account of the balance of payments.

▶ A higher rate of inflation tends to drive up the nominal rate of interest (even if the real rate remains negative). The effect is to discourage investment by firms and also to persuade consumers to postpone purchases of consumer durables.

▶ Unemployment, however, also imposes costs on society. When there are unemployed workers in the economy, the actual output produced is below the potential output that can be produced from the available resources. This implies that the level of consumption available to society is less than could be achieved if all resources were employed. The more a nation produces, the more it can consume!

▶ There is a loss of revenue to the exchequer from lower tax revenues and increased expenditure on social security payments to the unemployed.

▶ If unemployment is severe enough, the profits of firms might fall and this is likely to depress investment. To the extent that investment raises productivity and reduces costs, living standards in the future will be lower than might otherwise have been achieved and domestic goods will become less competitive as compared with foreign goods.

▶ Unemployment is sometimes categorized by type:

  – **Frictional unemployment** occurs as a result of workers changing jobs. Over time, some workers will become unemployed and will not gain employment until they acquire new skills or move to different parts of the country. The fact that workers are mobile is a sign of a healthy economy, and the shorter the duration of frictional unemployment, the healthier the economy.

  – **Structural unemployment** occurs when there is a change in the structure of demand because patterns of consumption change. The problem is that industries are sometimes highly localized, so that structural unemployment is often synonymous with **regional unemployment**.

  – **Cyclical unemployment** occurs as a result of regular and recurring changes in economic activity known as the **trade cycle**. In the upswing of the cycle, unemployment falls, and during the downswing, unemployment rises.

  – **Seasonal unemployment** occurs as a result of changes in the seasons. More people are employed in agriculture in the summer months than in the winter months, for example.

  – **Real wage unemployment** is the level of unemployment that exists when output is at the natural rate.

▶ The existence of a natural rate of unemployment as the equilibrium rate implies that unemployment will only fall permanently below the natural rate if there is a permanent reduction in the real wage. As real wages fall, real profits will rise, and this provides an incentive for firms to increase output and recruit more workers.

▶ The existence of a natural rate of unemployment does *not* imply that governments are powerless to reduce unemployment. It simply implies that they are powerless to bring about a permanent reduction in unemployment by increasing aggregate demand.

▶ Unemployment can only be reduced in the long run if there is a reduction in the natural rate.

▶ The natural rate of unemployment is determined by such factors as the rate of technological progress, the mobility of labour, the existence of minimum wage legislation, the existence of restrictions on competition in markets, and so on.

▶ To reduce the natural rate of unemployment, governments the world over have introduced **supply-side policies** aimed at improving the efficiency with which markets work in the belief that this will stimulate employment.

▶ Supply-side policies include: **deregulation**, that is, freeing markets from regulations which restrict competition and **privatization**. Privatization involves a change of ownership and, arguably, increases incentives (via profit to owners) to meet consumer needs, etc. Legislation aimed at reducing the power of trade unions and tax reductions to increase incentives are also regarded as supply-side policies (see pp. 62–63).

★ REVISION ACTIVITIES

1 Why might inflation be less of a problem if it is stable and predictable from one year to the next than if it is variable and unpredictable?

2 Why does an increase in the rate of money growth cause inflation?

3   If the velocity of circulation is constant, what does this imply about the demand
    for money?
4   If the rate of inflation is falling, why is the labour market in disequilibrium?

PRACTICE QUESTIONS

Question 1
Use aggregate demand and aggregate supply analysis to evaluate the relative
merits of reductions in income tax rates, compared with reductions in
unemployment benefits, as methods of reducing unemployment.

UODLE

Question 2

(a) Outline the main changes in unemployment which have occurred in the UK in
    the last ten years. [*12 marks*]
(b) Discuss the economic significance of this change in the pattern of employment.
    [*13 marks*]

AEB

Question 3
Monetarists and supply side economists believe that an economy has a natural
rate of unemployment.

(a) (i) What is the natural rate of unemployment? [*5 marks*]
    (ii) What factors determine whether the natural rate of unemployment in an
         economy is likely to be high or low? [*7 marks*]
(b) Assess the significance of the 'natural rate of unemployment hypothesis' for the
    conduct of economic policy. [*13 marks*]

AEB

6 International issues

- ▶ Absolute advantage
- ▶ Capital account
- ▶ Comparative advantage
- ▶ Depreciation
- ▶ Fixed exchange rate
- ▶ Floating exchange rate
- ▶ Invisible trade

- ▶ Monetary union
- ▶ Official reserves
- ▶ Tariff
- ▶ Terms of trade
- ▶ Trade creation
- ▶ Trade diversion
- ▶ Visible trade

REVISION TIPS

In recent years, **regional trading blocs** have become increasingly common as countries exploit their relative advantages. It is therefore important to be clear about the distinction between **trade creation** and **trade diversion** (see p. 88).

You also need to be clear about the different components of the **balance of payments** and the ways in which they are related. The distinction between short-term flows and long-term flows on the capital account is particularly important, since this shows how a deficit on the current account is financed and therefore the sustainability of such a deficit. You should also ensure that you are familiar with the general state of the balance of payments over approximately the last decade, and the changes that have taken place in the composition of UK exports and imports over this period.

Be clear about the relative advantages of **fixed** and **floating exchange rates** and, in particular, the implications for the way in which domestic economic policy is conducted under different exchange rate regimes. This is one of the main issues to be considered in arguments about **monetary union** – issues which you must understand clearly because of the current importance attached to them. Again, make sure you are familiar with the general behaviour of the exchange rate over the last few years.

TOPIC OUTLINE

Absolute and comparative advantage

- ▶ Countries trade together for all sorts of reasons, but the principal reason is undoubtedly that some countries are more efficient at producing some goods than others.
- ▶ A country is said to have an **absolute advantage** in the production of a good when it can produce more of that good than another country with the same resource input.
- ▶ A country is said to have a **comparative advantage** in the production of a good when to produce an extra unit involves a smaller sacrifice of some other good, than is the case for another country. In other words, it has a *lower opportunity cost* in the production of one good as compared with another country.
- ▶ You can test your understanding of absolute and comparative advantage in the revision activities on p. 56.

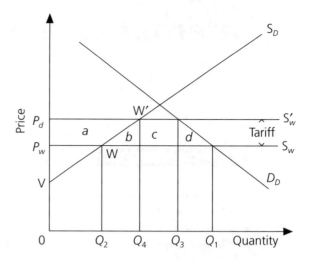

Figure 6.1 The effect of a tariff on price, quantity consumed and consumer welfare

Protection

- ▶ Despite the advantages of trade, countries sometimes **protect** their industries from competition.
- ▶ Protection can take a variety of forms, the most obvious being **tariffs** and **quotas**.
- ▶ Whatever form protection takes, the aim is always to divert demand away from imports in favour of domestic substitutes.
- ▶ The problem here is the implication that domestic producers are less efficient than foreign producers. There is a danger that by protecting domestic producers from competition any relative inefficiency may be perpetuated.
- ▶ The argument that **infant industries** should be protected is often advanced. Here protection is seen as temporary until such time as the 'infant' grows sufficiently to compete independently of any protection.
- ▶ A serious problem with protection is that it implies a suboptimal allocation of resources. This can be explained in terms of Figure 6.1, where S_D and D_D are the *domestic* supply and demand curves for a particular product. The world price of the product is P_w and, in the absence of a tariff, world supply of the product to the domestic economy is perfectly elastic at the ruling world price. This gives an effective supply curve to the domestic economy of VWS_w and an equilibrium quantity of Q_1, of which $Q_2 - Q_1$ is imported.
- ▶ Now assume a tariff is imposed on imports of this product equal to P_wP_d. The price of the product **in the domestic market** now rises to P_d, since the new world supply shifts upwards to S'_w. As a result, consumption from overseas falls by Q_1Q_3 but consumption of domestic output rises by Q_2Q_4.
- ▶ There is a **welfare loss** to society from the tariff. For example, the welfare loss to consumers is equal to the area $a + b + c + d$. However, the welfare gain to producers is equal to area a and the gain to the government in tax revenue is equal to area c. The net welfare loss to society is therefore area b plus area d.

The balance of payments

The current account

- ▶ The **current account** consists of two sub-accounts: the **visible account** and the **invisible account**.
- ▶ The visible account deals with trade in **goods**, and the invisible account deals with trade in **services**, flows of profits and remittances sent home by ex-patriots.
- ▶ The balance on the visible account plus the balance on the invisible account gives the balance on the overall current account.
- ▶ Typically, the UK has a deficit on the visible account, and a surplus on the invisible account that is less than the deficit on the visible account.

The capital account

▶ The **capital account** records flows of investment funds, changes in banks' holding of foreign currency, and changes in the **official reserves** of foreign currency.

▶ Any excess of expenditure on imports over revenue from exports must be matched by an equal excess of inflows of funds over outflows of funds on the capital account. Otherwise there will be a loss of official reserves etc. This is because, as an accounting identity, the overall balance of payments must be zero.

▶ Capital inflows might be short-term or long-term. Short-term inflows are attracted by a relatively higher interest rate differential available in the UK and are sometimes referred to as **hot money** because if there is a relative rise in interest rates abroad, these funds can quickly and easily be withdrawn.

▶ Long-term inflows of capital represent investment in equity in UK companies or in other securities with more than one year to run to maturity.

▶ Any deficit on the current account which is not offset by private flows of capital must be offset by changes in the official reserves of foreign currency.

The balance of trade and the terms of trade

▶ The **balance of trade** is simply another name for the **visible balance**.

▶ The **terms of trade** is an index of export prices divided by an index of import prices.

▶ An **improvement** in the terms of trade implies that there has been a rise in the terms of trade index: that is, export prices have risen relative to import prices.

▶ If there is an improvement in the UK's terms of trade, then one (or more) of three things has happened:

 – sterling has depreciated on the foreign exchanges;
 – the rate of inflation in the UK has been above that in other countries; or
 – prices in the UK have fallen by less than prices in other countries.

▶ There is not necessarily any direct relationship between changes in the terms of trade and changes in the balance of trade. Sometimes they move in the same direction, sometimes in opposite directions.

▶ The impact of a change in the terms of trade on the balance of trade depends partly on the price elasticities of demand for exports and imports (see p. 55).

Exchange rates

▶ **Exchange rates** are simply the price of two monies: that is, the price of one currency in terms of another. For example, if the sterling/dollar exchange rate is £1 = $1.67, this implies that each pound buys $1.67 dollars or one dollar buys about £0.60 (1/1.67).

▶ Exchange rates are determined by supply and demand for currency on the foreign exchange market. When supply and demand operate freely, exchange rates are said to **float**, and when the authorities intervene to influence supply and demand for currency, exchange rates are **administratively determined**.

▶ When the authorities allow only minor changes in the exchange rate, exchange rates are said to be **fixed**.

▶ Among the world's major currencies, the authorities tend to intervene to smooth adjustments in supply and demand: that is, they do not resist the general direction in which the market is moving the currency, but simply try to ensure that the currency moves in as smooth a way as possible.

▶ The main factor influencing the exchange rate in the long run is **relative inflation rates**.

▶ If one country has a higher rate of inflation than its trading partners, it will tend to import more than it exports, i.e. it will tend to have a current account deficit. If there is no intervention by the authorities, this will lead to a depreciation of the exchange rate: that is, the currency of the high-inflation country will buy less of other currencies.

▶ The relationship between the rate of inflation and the exchange rate is given by the **purchasing power parity theory**.

▶ In its strictest form, this theory states that exchange rates will adjust so that a consumer pays the same price for a basket of goods whether they are purchased in the domestic economy or from abroad.

▶ To ensure that this is the case, any rise in the relative price of a basket of goods purchased in the domestic economy must be offset by a depreciation of that currency on the foreign exchange market.

▶ Depreciation can be resisted by the authorities if they buy up the excess supply of domestic currency, i.e. sell foreign currency from the official reserves.

▶ This is only a short-run expedient since official holdings of foreign currency are limited.

▶ Usually, if the authorities wish to resist a depreciation of the exchange rate, they will raise the rate of interest in the domestic economy to attract capital inflows and reduce capital outflows.

▶ The *rate of interest* is therefore the main determinant of the exchange rate in the short run.

▶ Crucially, if the authorities raise the rate of interest to reduce downward pressure on the foreign exchange value of a currency, then they cannot simultaneously use changes in the rate of interest to achieve domestic policy aims. In other words there may be a conflict of objectives when using interest rate policy.

Fixed versus floating exchange rates

▶ The *advantages* of fixed exchange rates are the *disadvantages* of floating exchange rates.

▶ It is usually suggested that one of the main advantages of fixed exchange rates is that they provide stable exchange rates, so that firms are able to make plans about future sales and purchases internationally without the risk of frequent changes in the exchange rate.

▶ Another advantage of fixed exchange rates is that the authorities can intervene to smooth the effect of changes in the flow of funds that might otherwise cause fluctuations in the exchange rate, which might in turn result in still larger fluctuations because of speculative pressure.

▶ Another alleged advantage of fixed exchange rates is the *discipline* it necessitates! For example, because the authorities are compelled to preserve the external value of the currency, they are obliged to follow a non-inflationary domestic monetary policy. If they did not, rising domestic inflation would ultimately lead to a balance of payments deficit and downward pressure on the exchange rate.

▶ Initially, this might be countered by using the foreign exchange reserves to stabilize the exchange rate, but if downward pressure continued, the authorities would be compelled to take action in the domestic economy to curtail inflation.

▶ A significant advantage of floating exchange rates is that there is no need for intervention in the foreign exchange market. A balance of payments deficit or surplus is self-correcting through changes in the exchange rate. However, a necessary condition for this involves price elasticities of demand. The Marshall Lerner conditions state that the PED for exports + PED for imports must be >1 if the exchange rate is to correct a deficit or surplus (see p. 55).

▶ Because there is no need for intervention in the foreign exchange market, the authorities are free to set domestic policy in order to achieve their aims in the domestic economy.

▶ A possible problem with the authorities pursuing domestic policy aims is that the absence of an exchange rate constraint might encourage them to adopt a relatively inflationary policy stance.

The effect of depreciation on the balance of payments

▶ We have previously written that a current account deficit is associated with **depreciation** of the currency on the foreign exchange market.

▶ Sometimes this might be exactly what policy-makers wish to happen because it might remove the current account deficit.

▶ Depreciation **reduces the foreign price of exports** and **increases the domestic price of imports**.

▶ As the foreign price of exports *falls* they will become more competitive and more will be sold. Conversely, as the domestic price of imports *rises* their competitiveness will fall and less will be bought.

▶ The effect of these price changes on the current account depends on the price elasticity of demand for exports and the price elasticity of demand for imports.

▶ It is usually argued that so long as the **sum** of the elasticities of demand for exports and imports is **greater than 1** (the Marshall Lerner conditions discussed above), depreciation will improve the current account.

▶ In reality, there are other important variables that determine the effect of depreciation on the current account.

▶ There are **time lags** before the full effects of depreciation are manifested in changes in the current account. It takes time for patterns of consumption to alter, and so, after depreciation, much the same volume will be exported at a lower foreign price and much the same volume will be imported at a higher domestic price.

▶ Because of this, depreciation is likely to cause an initial increase in the size of the current account deficit. Whether depreciation is considered successful or not, therefore, partly depends on the time period under consideration.

▶ Depreciation causes important **income effects**. To the extent that exports increase and imports fall, national income will rise for the depreciating country, but it will fall in other countries as their own exports fall and imports rise.

▶ The full effect of this depends partly on the **income elasticity of demand for imports** in both countries. Depreciation has most chance of success if the income elasticity of demand for imports is low in the depreciating country and high in other countries. In this case the rise in national income in the depreciating country will have less impact in raising future imports, and the fall in national income overseas will have less impact in depressing its future exports.

▶ There might also be **supply bottlenecks** which restrict the ability of firms to respond to any increase in demand for its exports.

▶ For a country such as the UK with its high dependency on imports of raw materials, there is a possibility of an **increase in the rate of inflation** following depreciation, as imported raw material prices rise.

Monetary union

▶ Moves towards European Monetary Union (EMU) are gathering momentum and it is important to consider whether the UK should exercise its 'opt out' clause or should, in fact, 'opt in' to monetary union.

▶ Monetary union can be achieved if exchange rates are irrevocably locked together, but in the case of Europe, the ultimate aim is the establishment of a single common currency to be known as the **euro**.

▶ The single market was completed in 1992, and there is now free movement of goods, labour and capital within the EU. This has obvious benefits for all concerned, since resources are free to move to where they are most efficiently used and countries are able to specialize where they have greatest comparative advantage. The single market also encourages larger-scale production.

▶ However, it is argued by some that the benefits of the single market will never fully materialize until there is a single currency.

▶ One reason for this is that international trade currently involves exchanging currencies, which adds to the risk and expense of doing business abroad.

▶ If a single currency existed, both of these problems would disappear, and the increase in trade as a result of this has been estimated as being in the order of 5–10 per cent of Community GNP.

▶ It is also estimated that further savings of about 0.5 per cent of Community GNP would be achieved with a single currency from the elimination of foreign exchange transactions costs.

▶ One problem with entering a monetary union is that if a single currency existed, monetary policy would be set for the whole of the European Union, and therefore an individual country loses the ability to set its own monetary policy.

▶ Loss of policy sovereignty over monetary policy implies that a country must accept whatever monetary policy is deemed desirable for the Union as a whole, even though this might not be the most appropriate policy for each individual country in the Union. An inappropriate level of money supply or interest rate can clearly cause serious domestic problems.

▶ Not only is sovereignty in monetary policy lost, the power to adjust the exchange rate for economic advantage is also lost.

▶ The exchange rate is a powerful instrument of economic management, and changes in the exchange rate can have profound effects on the domestic economy.

▶ Care must be taken not to exaggerate the importance of losing this policy instrument, though, because the absence of capital controls has already restricted the ability of the authorities to vary the exchange rate.

▶ There would, of course, be costs associated with introducing a new currency. It has been estimated that changing computer programs alone (to facilitate pricing in euros) would involve a cost of some £500m.

★ REVISION ACTIVITIES

1 The following table shows the units of resources required to produce one unit of food or one unit of clothing in two countries:

	Units of resources required	
	Per one unit of food	Per one unit of clothing
Country A	4	6
Country B	4	8

(a) Which country has an absolute advantage in the production of clothing?
(b) Which country has a comparative advantage in the production of food?

2 Consider the following information:

	Rate of tariff		
	0	4	6
Cost of wheat in:			
Country A	10	10	10
Country B (before customs union)	8	12	14
Country B (after customs union)	8	8	8
Country C	5	9	11

(a) Assume that there is initially no customs union.
  (i) If country A has an initial tariff of 4 on all imports of wheat, from which country will it obtain its supplies of wheat?
  (ii) If, instead, country A has an initial tariff of 6 on all imports of wheat, from which country will it now obtain its supplies of wheat?

(b) Assume countries A and B now form a customs union. Show how, if country A maintains its tariff of 6 against imports of wheat from outside the union, trade will be created, but that if Country A sets its tariff against imports of wheat at 4, trade will be diverted.

PRACTICE QUESTIONS

Question 1

Freeing world trade – the Uruguay Round of the GATT talks

In 1947, twenty-seven nations signed the GATT agreement. There are now 120 members. The agreement is aimed at preventing any increase in restrictions to world trade and reducing present overt and covert barriers through negotiation. The Uruguay Round of talks commenced in 1986 and were finally concluded in 1993. As Figure 6.2 illustrates, it included in its remit subsidies to financial services, intellectual property and the film industry, along with the usual targets such as agriculture and textiles.

The agreement amounts to a move towards the target of free world trade and should promote a 1 per cent growth in total world output. However, in some countries, industries may lose out in the short run from freer trade, and these losses need to be considered before a final assessment of the overall benefits of the latest GATT agreement can be made.

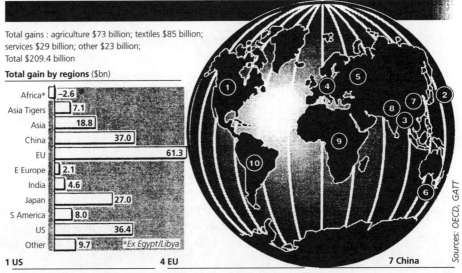

Total gains : agriculture $73 billion; textiles $85 billion; services $29 billion; other $23 billion; Total $209.4 billion

Total gain by regions ($bn)

Africa*	–2.6
Asia Tigers	7.1
Asia	18.8
China	37.0
EU	61.3
E Europe	2.1
India	4.6
Japan	27.0
S America	8.0
US	36.4
Other	9.7 *Ex Egypt/Libya

Sources: OECD, GATT

1 US

Largest number of world's 500 biggest global companies, and biggest services exporter ($2 billion benefit). Aerospace, computer software, agriculture ($9.3 billion) and textile ($21.6 billion) sectors will also benefit. Total gain: $36 billion a year by 2002.

2 Japan

Set to gain from liberalisation in high-tech goods, agriculture ($22 billion), manufacturing. Loses $0.5 billion through textile liberalization. Total gain $27 billion a year by 2002.

3 Asian Tigers

Gain $3.3 billion through farm liberalization, $1.8 billion in textiles, $1.1 billion in services. $7.1 billion overall gain.

4 EU

World's biggest exporting block. Agriculture to see income increase of $30 billion, textiles ($17.2 billion), services ($7 billion), manufacturing ($7.6 billion) all set to gain – but prospects differ in each country. Total gain: $61.3 billion a year by 2002.

5 Eastern Europe

Textile, service sectors likely to benefit. Former Soviet Union set to gain by some $13 billion from liberalization of services. Total gain: $37 billion a year by 2002.

6 Australia/New Zealand

Large gains from liberalization of agriculture ($1.0 billion), textile ($1.1 billion). Total gain: $2 billion a year by 2002.

7 China

Set to gain $37 billion a year by 2002.

8 India

Set to gain $4.6 billion a year by 2002.

9 Africa (excluding Egypt and Libya)

The continent as a whole is set to lose $2.6 billion, with Nigeria alone down $1.0 billion. Morocco, Algeria and Tunisia together lose $0.6 billion, and South Africa loses $0.4 billion.

10 South America

Set to gain $8.0 billion, with Brazil on its own up $3.4 billion. *The estimates also take no account of external costs arising from the structural adjustment of economies in the wake of trade liberalization.*

Figure 6.2 GATT: who wins what

Study the data and answer the following questions.

(a) (i) What do the initials GATT stand for? [*1 mark*]
　　(ii) Give *one* example of overt and *one* example of covert barriers to trade. [*2 marks*]
　　(iii) List *two* reasons why countries erect barriers to trade. [*2 marks*]
(b) (i) According to economic theory, what are the main advantages of free trade? Does the data in any way support this view? [*4 marks*]
　　(ii) Identify *two* trading areas which have the advantage in textiles production. Suggest reasons why this may be the case. [*4 marks*]
　　(iii) Using the US gains as the basis for comparison, create an index to show the financial gains from the GATT agreement for each of the following groups of countries:
　　　▶ Asia, Asia Tigers, China and India;
　　　▶ South America; and
　　　▶ Eastern Europe and the EU. [*4 marks*]
　　(iv) Using the table 'total gain by regions', evaluate whether the gains from GATT were greater for the industrialized countries or the developing countries. [*3 marks*]
(c) (i) Explain the following terms which are used at the bottom of the chart:
　　　▶ 'structural adjustment of economies'; and
　　　▶ 'external costs'. [*4 marks*]
　　(ii) Describe three external costs which might arise when structural adjustment takes place. [*6 marks*]

NICCEA

Question 2

(a) In what ways has economic integration already occurred in the European Union? [*12 marks*]
(b) Assess the economic issues involved in determining the future form of economic integration in the European Union. [*13 marks*]

UCLES

Question 3

(a) Explain the difference between a fixed exchange rate and a freely floating exchange rate. [*5 marks*]
(b) The exchange rate mechanism (ERM) of the European Monetary System was designed as a cross between fixed and floating rates. Explain how such a system works, and discuss the impact on the UK of leaving the ERM in September 1992. [*10 marks*]
(c) Explain why depreciation of a country's currency may, initially, cause the trade balance of that country to worsen, although eventually it will usually improve. [*10 marks*]

NICCEA

7 Domestic economic policy: aims and instruments

- ▶ Budget
- ▶ Central bank
- ▶ Central Government
- ▶ Direct taxation
- ▶ Discount market
- ▶ Economic growth
- ▶ Fiscal policy
- ▶ Incomes policy

- ▶ Indirect taxation
- ▶ Monetary policy
- ▶ Open market operations
- ▶ Public sector borrowing requirement
- ▶ Rate of interest
- ▶ Treasury bill
- ▶ Underground economy

REVISION TIPS

Domestic economic policy is a wide-ranging topic that draws on knowledge from across the whole area of macroeconomics. You need to understand basic macroeconomic theory (especially as outlined in Chapters 4 and 6), together with the aims, methods and consequences of different policy actions by the authorities and the ways in which different policies affect the different macroeconomic aggregates. It is also very important to be familiar with the conduct of economic policy in the recent past and to know how the different economic aggregates have changed in recent years.

TOPIC OUTLINE

The aims of economic policy

- ▶ In recent years the overriding aim of economic policy in the UK (and most of the developed countries) has been to achieve a relatively low rate of inflation.
- ▶ The long-term aim of policy has therefore been **price stability**.
- ▶ Countries are also concerned to increase their rate of **economic growth**. This is dealt with in Chapter 8.
- ▶ Another major aim of governments is to achieve as low a rate of inflation as is consistent with economic growth.
- ▶ Governments are also concerned to achieve a sustainable **balance of payments** position, and this implies that exports should roughly match imports in the long run.
- ▶ These aims are not mutually exclusive. For example, we have seen in Chapter 4 that an unanticipated increase in the rate of inflation can lead to an increase in economic activity and higher economic growth.
- ▶ However, a higher rate of inflation, whether anticipated or not, also leads to a deterioration of the current account and/or downward pressure on the exchange rate.

The instruments of economic policy

Monetary policy

▶ Monetary policy refers to controlling the rate at which the **money supply** grows (money growth).

▶ Various techniques are available for *controlling* money growth, but the most widely used technique is to vary the **rate of interest**.

▶ So-called **direct controls** that limit the growth of bank lending have proved ineffective in restraining money growth.

▶ The history of direct controls the world over is that if institutions require extra funds, then the financial institutions will find ways of circumventing any restrictions on their ability to meet any unfulfilled loan demand.

▶ This often means that loan demand is met through channels not subject to direct controls.

▶ Such channels are invariably less efficient than the institutions to which controls apply, and this constitutes a powerful case against the use of direct controls to restrict money growth, since business is transferred from more efficient institutions to less efficient institutions.

▶ Varying the rate of interest is a more effective technique of controlling money growth since interest-rate changes affect all institutions simultaneously and to the same extent.

▶ For example, if the authorities wish to engineer a contraction of money growth, this can most effectively be achieved by a rise in the rate of interest.

▶ The basic technique by which the authorities engineer a rise in interest rates is through their **open-market operations**.

▶ An open-market sale of securities by the Bank of England leads to a reduction in banks' operational deposits at the Bank of England.

▶ To restore these deposits to the desired level, banks call in their loans to other institutions, particularly their **call money** placed with the **discount market**.

▶ Since all institutions will be doing the same thing, the discount market will find itself short of funds and will be compelled to borrow from the Bank of England.

▶ All the Bank has to do is to increase the rate at which it lends to the discount market.

▶ The discount market will then be compelled to *increase* its own dealing rates (or else it will operate at a loss).

▶ In turn, other financial institutions will increase their own rates of interest, and so the Bank has achieved its aim.

Fiscal policy

▶ Fiscal policy is about government expenditure, and revenue from taxation, fees and the sale of assets.

▶ The main instrument of fiscal policy is the central government's budget, which is presented annually to Parliament in November.

▶ This is the occasion when the Chancellor of the Exchequer announces the government's expenditure and revenue plans for the forthcoming year.

▶ If government revenue *exceeds* expenditure there is a **budget surplus**, and if government revenue *is less than* expenditure, there is a **budget deficit**. The budget is **balanced** when government expenditure *equals* revenue.

▶ In general, there is a budget deficit in the UK, but the magnitude of the deficit varies.

▶ The size of the budget deficit is important for several reasons, but crucially because of its impact on aggregate demand and, depending on how the deficit is financed, because of its impact on money growth.

▶ A budget deficit implies an **increase in aggregate demand** since there is a net increase in expenditure over tax revenue, and this implies a short-run increase in output, employment and the price level.

▶ However, as output and employment return to the **natural rate**, the increase in aggregate demand results only in a rise in the price level.

▶ The budget deficit is now considered more important because of its impact on money growth, rather than because of its impact on aggregate demand.

▶ The budget deficit is the main component of the **public sector borrowing requirement (PSBR)**. The other components are the **local authority borrowing requirement** and the **borrowing requirement of the public corporations**.

▶ In comparison with the central government's budget deficit, neither of the other two components of the PSBR is considered significant.

▶ For this reason, the term '**budget deficit**' is sometimes used synonymously with the **PSBR**. This convention is followed here.

Financing the budget deficit

▶ The budget deficit must be financed by government borrowing, and the way in which this borrowing is conducted has implications for money growth.

▶ When the government borrows, it issues securities such as **Treasury bills** in return for funds. Government securities can therefore be thought of as IOUs.

▶ If the government borrows from the **non-bank private sector**, deposits are transferred from the private sector to the public sector and then returned to the private sector when borrowed funds are spent. The net change in money growth in these circumstances is zero.

▶ The situation is different if the government borrows from the **banking sector**. In this case, securities are purchased by the banking sector which thereby creates additional deposits with itself, and therefore each deposit created as a result of purchasing government debt is a one-for-one increase in the money supply.

▶ The greater the amount of government borrowing financed through the **monetary sector** as a whole, the greater the impact of government borrowing on money growth.

▶ The government might also borrow from **overseas** or in **foreign currency**.

▶ If the government borrows from overseas or in foreign currency, money growth rises by the full amount of government borrowing as the borrowed funds are spent.

▶ There might also be a secondary expansionary effect because the monetary sector will acquire additional liquidity (i.e. the monetary base will rise), and this might lead to a multiple expansion of bank lending.

Discretionary policy

▶ Governments have sometimes adopted a **discretionary** approach to economic policy.

▶ This implies a counter-cyclical policy. In the downswing of the cycle, expansionary monetary and (especially) fiscal policies are implemented with the aim of boosting aggregate demand so that output and employment rise.

▶ In the upswing of the cycle, contractionary monetary and (especially) fiscal policies are implemented so as to reduce aggregate demand and reign back inflationary pressure.

▶ This is sometimes referred to as **stabilization policy**.

Targeting the money supply

▶ It is often suggested that governments should aim at sustaining a steady rate of growth of the money supply in order to achieve a stable rate of inflation. The basic idea is that if money growth is at a constant rate, this provides information to the private sector about future inflation, which can be taken into account by those involved in fixing wages and prices.

▶ A stable rate of growth of the money supply also provides a self-correcting mechanism for dealing with changes in the level of economic activity.

▶ During a recession, the supply of money will rise at the target rate but demand for money will fall. This implies an excess supply of money, which will lead to increased expenditures. During a boom, the opposite happens.

▶ If governments pursue a target rate of growth for the money supply, they relinquish the use of discretionary policy to deal with shocks (e.g. an oil price rise) that might otherwise lead to an increase in unemployment as output falls.

▶ In other words, there is an acceptance that the market is better able to achieve stability than intervention by the authorities.

▶ The problem with discretionary policies is that they generate unanticipated inflation and lead to inefficiency in the allocation of resources (see p. 48).

An independent central bank

▶ If it is accepted that discretionary changes in monetary policy are undesirable, the problem is how to achieve stability in money growth and how to convince the private sector that such stability will be maintained.

▶ It is not sufficient for the government simply to announce that it is to follow some target rate of growth for the money supply for the foreseeable future. If governments have been unreliable in achieving the policy pronouncements in the past, future policy pronouncements will have little credibility. This is important because if the private sector does not believe governments will deliver their policy promises, such policy promises will not achieve the desired results.

▶ One way in which credibility in monetary policy can be achieved is to create an **independent central bank**.

▶ The present arrangements in the UK are such that the Bank of England automatically finances the government's overdraft and this limits the extent to which the Bank can control money growth.

▶ If the central bank *is* independent, it can be charged with the responsibility of preserving the internal value of the currency, as in the case of Germany's Bundesbank.

▶ The success of the Bundesbank (and other independent central banks, such as that of New Zealand) in achieving relative price stability encourages the belief that independent central banks can deliver price stability.

▶ The policy statements from an independent central bank would also have more credibility than policy statements from a government that might have political reasons for engineering an upturn in economic activity.

▶ An independent central bank could take a long-run view of policy and would set the target rate of growth for the money supply accordingly. A government, compelled to face the electorate at some point, might take a shorter-term view and implement a suboptimal target.

▶ An independent national central bank is also essential if the proposed European Central Bank is to be independent, as proposed by the Treaty of Maastricht.

Supply-side policies

▶ The failure of stabilization policies – which aim to bring about changes in macroeconomic aggregates by altering aggregate demand – to deliver long-run success has led to a shift of emphasis away from demand-side policies in favour of supply-side policies.

▶ The aim of supply-side policies is to shift the short-run aggregate supply curve downwards and to the right and to shift the long-run aggregate supply curve to the right by increasing productivity, that is, by using resources more efficiently.

▶ The effect of this on output and the price level is illustrated in Figure 7.1, where AD_0 is the aggregate demand curve, AS_{S0} is the initial short-run aggregate supply curve and AS_{L0} is the initial long-run aggregate supply curve.

▶ In equilibrium, the initial price level is P_0 and the initial level of output is Y_0.

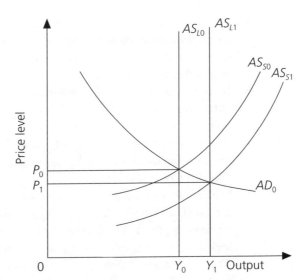

Figure 7.1 The effect of an increase in productivity on output and price

- If supply-side policies are successful, the short-run aggregate supply curve shifts downwards to AS_{S1} and the long-run aggregate supply curve shifts to the right to AS_{L1}.
- The equilibrium price level falls to P_1 and the level of output rises to Y_1.
- The potential impact on the standard of living, employment and on the rate of inflation of successful supply side policies is clear.
- Supply-side policies can take many forms. However, one important approach is to devise policies which encourage incentives.
- In the labour market, incentives can most obviously be improved by reducing rates of income tax. In the 1980s, it was estimated that almost two million people were either better off or no worse off if they were unemployed that if they were employed. This situation was due to the way in which the tax and benefit systems operate: that is, relatively high marginal rates of taxation, relatively low tax-free allowances, and early withdrawal of benefit when earnings rise.
- To reduce the extent of this **unemployment trap** and to provide an incentive for the unemployed to accept job offers, marginal rates of income tax have been lowered and there are plans for further reductions.
- **Privatization** and **deregulation** are also supply-side policies designed to improve the efficiency with which markets operate (see pp. 27–28).
- The government has also introduced a **job seekers' allowance** for the unemployed. To qualify for benefit, individuals must be able to demonstrate that they are actively seeking work and not passively waiting for job opportunities to come their way.
- There have also been measures to restrict the power of the trade unions to disrupt production in furtherance of a dispute: mass picketing and secondary picketing are no longer allowed; trade union members must be given a vote and a majority must vote in favour of strike action before such action can be called; trade unions have lost their immunity from prosecution for damages as a result of industrial action, and so on.
- Partly as a result of trade union legislation, membership of unions is now falling, and there have been unprecedented changes in working practices that have to some extent been responsible for the rapid rise in labour productivity in the UK in recent years.

Incomes policy

- One approach to economic policy that has been used on several occasions in the UK is an **incomes policy**. It is anticipated that by limiting the growth of incomes, pressure on prices will be reduced and the rate of inflation will fall.

- Sometimes incomes policy is linked to a policy on prices, in which case we refer to a **prices and incomes policy**. By linking limits on pay increases to limits on price increases, it is anticipated that limiting wage increases will be more acceptable to the labour force.
- Incomes policies might be **voluntary** or **compulsory**. Neither policy has been particularly successful in controlling inflation in the long run, though compulsory policies have had limited short-run success.
- A serious problem with any policy that limits prices and/or incomes is that it prevents the market from discharging its role efficiently and therefore impairs the allocation of resources.
- With respect to the labour market, by restricting wage increases, growth industries are prevented from offering the higher wages necessary to attract the skilled workers required. The incentive for those employed in contracting industries to seek alternative employment is also diminished.
- The implication is that an incomes policy might reduce economic growth (see p. 68) and lead to higher unemployment in future years.
- One possible way to avoid this problem is to allow wage increases that are linked in some way to productivity increases.
- Growth industries will experience rising productivity, and this will allow them to offer higher wages.
- The problem with this approach is that the productivity of some groups, particularly those in the service sector, cannot easily be measured.
- Because of this problem, productivity increases might still not achieve the desired result, and, in any case, they tend to be resented because of the perception that they are in some sense unfair.
- Despite these arguments, it is widely believed that the chief problem with incomes policies is that they do not operate on the primary cause of inflation, i.e. excessive money growth.
- Incomes policy might well restrict the growth of wages, but if money growth continues unabated, prices will go on rising and real income will simply be distributed away from those whose incomes are subject to the controls in favour of those who receive incomes which are not, especially profits.

Switching the balance between direct and indirect taxes

- Politicians often state their desire to shift the burden of taxation away from **direct taxes**, particularly personal income tax, in favour of **indirect taxes**.
- Probably the main economic reason for politicians' interest in reducing the burden of direct taxes, such as personal income tax, is because of the widely held view that relatively high rates of income tax are a disincentive to effort and initiative.

  As previously argued on p. 41, many people can be caught in the unemployment trap. If personal income tax is reduced in favour of higher indirect taxes, the extent of this problem would fall.
- Another possibility is that relatively high rates of direct taxation encourage the growth of the underground or 'black' economy. Reducing the burden of direct taxation might therefore help reverse this trend.

  Estimates of the size of the 'black' economy in the UK range from 2 per cent to 14 per cent of GNP. A reduction in direct taxation, by reducing the benefits accruing from tax evasion, might reduce the extent of the underground economy.
- To the degree that this occurs, it might be possible to reduce the overall burden of taxation without reducing tax revenue.
- A primary advantage of indirect taxation over direct taxation is that indirect taxes can be applied selectively.
- This might be particularly useful in dealing with negative externalities (see p. 31) and, to the extent that indirect taxes are placed on those activities which generate negative externalities, resource allocation will be improved.

► Moreover, it is possible that relatively high rates of direct taxation, by reducing personal disposable income, also reduce the amount of savings in the economy. This seems even more likely because interest income is also subject to income tax. On the other hand a greater use of indirect taxation may stimulate savings.

► Any increase in the flow of savings will raise the amount available for investment, and this has implications for the rate of economic growth.

► Despite the points above, direct taxes provide a powerful means of affecting aggregate demand in the short-run. Indirect taxes probably exert their influence over a longer period of time.

► This implies that price changes via indirect taxes have less of an immediate impact on consumption – and therefore on aggregate demand – than do changes in income via direct taxes, perhaps because indirect taxes are spread over a wider area.

► Direct taxes are also more powerful in bringing about changes in the distribution of income. Indirect taxes tend to operate **regressively**: that is, those on lower incomes pay a higher proportion of their income in taxes than those on higher incomes. Direct taxes, on the other hand, can be structured in a **progressive** way so that the marginal rate of tax exceeds the average rate of tax.

► Personal income tax is an example of a progressive tax because, as income rises and income earners enter higher tax bands, the marginal rate of tax rises.

REVISION ACTIVITIES

1 If the PSBR has a fixed target value, what does this imply about the conduct of economic policy?

2 How is a relatively large and unexpected increase in the size of the central government's budget deficit likely to affect interest rates?

3 Why are changes in GDP more useful in measuring changes in productivity than changes in GNP.

PRACTICE QUESTIONS

Question 1
Study Table 7.1 and, using your knowledge of economics, answer the questions which follow.

(a) With reference to the data in the table, examine the relationship between the trends in unemployment and:
   (i) nominal GDP; [*2 marks*]
   (ii) real GDP. [*2 marks*]
(b) Which of the GDP measures in part (a) provides a better insight into the behaviour of unemployment during this period? Explain why this is so. [*3 marks*]
(c) (i) How are changes in the level of economic activity likely to affect the PSBR? Carefully explain your answer. [*6 marks*]
   (ii) To what extent do the data provide support for your answer to (c)(i)? [*9 marks*]
(d) Excluding any which you may have already mentioned, identify and comment on *one* additional factor which could affect the size of the PSBR. [*3 marks*]

UODLE

Question 2

(a) How can the government influence the level of interest rates? [*12 marks*]
(b) Discuss the likely effects of a significant increase in interest rates upon the rate of inflation. [*13 marks*]

AEB

Table 7.1   The economic cycle and the PSBR

Year	Nominal GDP (£bn)	Real GDP (£bn)	Unemployment rate (%)	PSBR* (£bn)	Government income from taxes and social security contributions (% change †)	Government expenditure on social security benefits (% change †)
	(1)	(2)	(3)	(4)	(5)	(6)
1986	328.3	320.2	11.1	2.4	5.8	8.6
1987	360.7	335.1	10.0	−1.3	8.7	2.7
1988	401.4	351.6	8.0	−11.9	11.0	2.6
1989	441.8	359.5	6.2	−9.3	7.8	4.4
1990	478.9	361.5	5.8	−2.3	7.9	8.7
1991	495.9	354.0	8.0	7.7	2.8	17.3
1992	516.5	352.2	9.7	28.6	0.2	14.8
1993	546.7	360.0	10.3	42.5	2.5	8.7
1994	579.1	374.2	9.4	37.1	7.8	3.6

Notes: Excepting columns 2 and 3, all data are given in, or based on, current prices. Column 2 is constant price data related to 1985.

* The PSBR records the excess of expenditures for current and capital purposes of the government and public corporations over all their current revenue.

† Percentage change on previous year.

Source: Adapted from *United Kingdom National Accounts, 1995* and *Economic Trends, 1995,* Crown copyright 1995. Reproduced by the permission of the Controller of HMSO and the Central Statistical Office.

Question 3

(a) What is meant by 'interest rates'? Explain the difference between 'nominal rate of interest' and 'real rate of interest'. [*5 marks*]

(b) Show how a change in interest rates can affect the equilibrium level of national income in an economy. [*10 marks*]

(c) Discuss the case for and against interest rates being under the control of an independent central bank. [*10 marks*]

NICCEA

8 Economic growth and development

- Economic aid
- Gross national product
- International debt

- Per capita income
- Standard of living
- Vicious circle of poverty

REVISION TIPS

Economic growth is sometimes defined as an **increase in real gross national product (GNP)** and sometimes as an **increase in real GNP per capita**. The latter is the most commonly used measure of the standard of living because it represents real GNP per head of population. Note that these aggregates do not necessarily move in the same direction. It is possible for one of these aggregates to change while the other is constant or, indeed, for both aggregates to move in opposite directions.

Economists define levels of **development** in terms of per capita income, but there are no hard and fast rules about what constitutes a developed country and what constitutes a less developed country. Most of the developed countries are industrialized economies, but some countries with a relatively high per capita income, such as Saudi Arabia, rely on oil for their wealth. To analyse the problems of any developing country, take care to consider the characteristics of its economy!

TOPIC OUTLINE

Economic growth

- The earliest theory of economic growth was that put forward by Malthus at the turn of the eighteenth century. Malthus argued that each country had a fixed amount of productive resources and that this determined the level of output in the long run.
- He argued that population growth would lead to famine and starvation as the available food supply and other resources dwindled and had to be shared among an ever larger number of people. This would provide a brake on population growth.
- Malthus's analysis gave economics its epithet, 'The Dismal Science'. Yet it is easy to dismiss the predictions of Malthus because, for the developed world, additional resources have been discovered and the productivity of resources has increased many times over. Since the time of Malthus, therefore, population growth has actually accompanied a rising standard of living.
- In more recent years, advances in birth control have given an element of choice to reproduction. Indeed, in the 1990s, the populations of several developed countries have actually fallen and are set to go on falling into the foreseeable future.
- However, for many of the world's poorer countries, the real Malthusian trap has been sprung because population growth has exceeded the growth of output, and in these countries, famine is an everyday reality for millions of people.

Table 8.1   Sources of growth in the United States, 1929–82

Sources of growth	Contribution to growth rate (%)	
Extensive growth		
Labour inputs	0.93	
Capital inputs	0.55	1.48
Intensive growth		
Education per worker	0.41	
Advances in knowledge	0.81	
Improved resource allocation	0.23	
Economies of scale	0.26	1.71
Other		−0.26
Overall growth		2.90

Source: E.F. Denison, *Trends in American Economic Growth, 1929–1982*, The Brookings
Institution, 1985.

▶ There are various factors that influence economic growth. One attempt to assess
the relative importance of such factors in generating economic growth in the USA
over some fifty years is given in Table 8.1.

▶ **Extensive growth** refers to growth in output resulting from increases in the
quantity of inputs, while **intensive growth** refers to growth in output resulting
from increases in the *quality* of inputs.

The standard of living

▶ Economic growth is important because of its effect on the **standard of living**.

▶ The standard of living is a difficult concept to define since there are all sorts of
non-quantifiable factors (e.g. the degree of political freedom) that strictly ought to
be considered when assessing the standard of living.

▶ Nevertheless, one factor that has an important influence on the standard of living
is the amount of output the population can consume. If all other things are equal,
the more we consume, the higher our standard of living.

▶ The most widely used measure of the standard of living is real GNP per capita.
This is simply GNP (after allowing for inflation) divided by population. Therefore
the change in living standards between one period and another is given by the
differences in the growth of real GNP and in the growth of population.

▶ Despite its widespread use, real GNP per capita is an imperfect measure of the
standard of living. It must therefore be used with caution when comparing
changes in the standard of living over time in a country or when making
comparisons between countries (see pp. 113–114).

▶ When real GNP per capita is used to compare changes in the standard of living
over time in a country, care must be taken to ensure that GNP has been measured
at *constant prices*, rather than at market (nominal) prices.

▶ Real GNP per capita might be reasonably constant between two periods, but the
total number of hours worked might have fallen, perhaps because of a reduction
in the number of hours worked per week or because there are more public
holidays than previously.

▶ Again there might have been changes in the volume of non-market output
produced between the two periods. For example, if more work is carried out on a
DIY basis, this will not be reflected in measures of GNP.

▶ Measures of GNP do not distinguish between the different types of output
produced and consumed. Yet it is the level of consumption which most affects the
standard of living in a given period. However, a rise in real GNP caused by an
increase in investment and/or an increase in the volume of exports will reduce the

amount available for domestic consumption. Thus again, real GNP per capita might fail to measure accurately changes in the standard of living.

Economic growth and the environment

▶ It is sometimes suggested that greater economic growth causes environmental degradation: more resources are extracted, more trees cut down and greater levels of pollution generated.
▶ This might be true in certain cases, but greater economic growth also implies a greater ability to replenish renewable resources (e.g. forests), clean up the environment, and so on.
▶ In general, economic growth in the West has outstripped growth in Eastern Europe, but it is Eastern Europe that has experienced the greatest environmental degradation.

Development

▶ Economic development is an impossible term to define precisely, but in broad terms it refers to the degree of industrialization and the level of GNP per capita.
▶ Those countries with the lowest GNP per capita are referred to as **less developed countries**. Economists then define **middle-income developing countries**, **high-income oil exporters** and **industrial market economies**.
▶ The main problem facing the developing countries is **poverty**, caused by a slow rate of economic growth of output and rapid population growth. Compared with developed economies, life expectancy is low, standards of literacy are low and infant mortality is high.
▶ Slow output growth is explained because many of the developing countries have a high dependency on subsistence agriculture where productivity grows only slowly.
▶ Income is often so low that it is difficult to save, and consequently there is little investment which might promote growth. This is the **vicious circle of poverty**.
▶ Population growth is a feature of many developing countries. There is no welfare system in these countries, and so children provide security in old age. Birth control advice and facilities may also be lacking.
▶ The income gap between the world's richest and the world's poorest countries is vast. For example, GNP per capita in the UK is nearly fifty times greater than GNP per capita in Ethiopia.
▶ The problem of poverty in the world's poorest countries is made worse by the degree of inequality between the wealthiest members of society and the poorest members. In Brazil, for example, the wealthiest 10 per cent of the population receive over 50 per cent of total income.

Strategies for development

Balanced or unbalanced growth

▶ Balanced growth implies that investment is increased across a broad range of sectors, so that all sectors of the economy grow at roughly the same rate.
▶ Proponents of this view argue that for any individual sector to grow, *all* sectors must grow.
▶ If only one sector grows, the growth of demand for its output will be limited and thus its growth potential will be limited.
▶ However, if all sectors grow, rising incomes ensure rising demand and an expanding market for the increased output of any sector.

▶ Proponents of unbalanced growth argue that balanced growth is not a feasible strategy, because it is impossible to generate the investment funds essential to increase investment across a broad range of sectors.

Trade or aid

▶ Aid is sometimes given by the developed world to the poorer countries in order to increase growth in those countries.

▶ While it is true that aid is given for altruistic reasons, it is also true that when poorer countries develop they will consume more products from the developed world and thus raise the income of the donor countries.

▶ It might be argued that aid provides poorer countries with the resources necessary to increase investment and enhance growth, ultimately to the benefit of the richer, exporting countries.

▶ A significant problem with aid is that it does not always involve the provision of the kind of resources that poorer countries require. In other words, inappropriate goods are sometimes despatched by donor countries to recipient countries.

▶ Even when financial aid is given (i.e. rather than in kind), there is still no guarantee that the aid will be used to acquire the resources most likely to promote growth. It might be spent on armaments, for example.

▶ As an alternative to aid, it is sometimes suggested that poorer countries should be given preferential trading opportunities so that markets are created for their products.

▶ Trade would encourage **export-led** growth and would enable poorer countries to increase their imports of capital and raw materials without running up as large a balance of payments deficit as they otherwise might.

▶ Trade would also encourage the development of the entrepreneurial talent that is necessary if economies are to grow. As export opportunities are created, profits from exporting will increase and entrepreneurs will respond accordingly.

International debt

▶ In the 1970s, many of the world's poorer countries began to build up substantial debt obligations to the richer countries.

▶ These debt obligations developed into the 'debt crisis' when recession in the richer countries led to a reduction in their imports from the poorer countries so that the latter could not 'service' their debt. In other words, the poorer countries were unable to meet their interest payments and/or repayment of debt.

▶ As the situation deteriorated, many debtor countries took the view that the only option was to **default**.

▶ When this happens with a domestic borrower some kind of collateral is usually called in by the banks to ensure that repayment obligations are met. In the case of a foreign government, however, this is virtually impossible, and so the banks were forced to **reschedule** debts: that is, to agree a new schedule of repayments.

▶ To assist the poorer countries, it was also agreed that part of their debt should be written off!

REVISION ACTIVITIES

1 Why is capital accumulation an important engine of economic growth?
2 Many of the world's poorer countries depend heavily on the export of primary products. What are primary products, and what problems are created by high dependency on them?

3 Is it true that poverty in the world's poorer countries has no economic significance for the world's richer countries?

PRACTICE QUESTIONS

Question 1

Economic development in Africa

For more than three decades the World Bank has shaped Africa's development, first, through large-scale projects and, more recently, through structural adjustment programmes (SAPs) designed with the International Monetary Fund. The record of environmental problems caused by the Bank has become widely known, but the failure of economic policies which has worsened poverty is one of the disasters of the post-war era.

Social and environmental problems have been compounded by economic failure. According to a 1992 World Bank report, around 60 per cent of its projects in Africa have failed to generate an economic return – a worse record than for any other developing region. But huge visible infrastructure projects are only a small part of the Bank's power on the continent.

The debt crisis of the 1980s extended the influence of the World Bank and the IMF into economic policy. Looming bankruptcy forced African governments to turn to the two agencies, whose seal of approval became a condition for western aid. In effect, the IMF assumed responsibility for budget policies, insisting on strict deflationary targets, and the World Bank oversaw moves towards trade liberalization and deregulation of agricultural markets.

The stated aim was to set Africa on the path to export-led recovery and, in the more recent pronouncements of the World Bank, to reduce poverty. The Bank was also aiming to reduce prices of agricultural exports: hence its encouragement to Latin American and Asian countries to compete with Africa in growing cocoa. Now, after a decade of adjustment, in which around thirty countries have followed World Bank and IMF advice, living standards in Africa have fallen by 2 per cent annually – and continue to fall.

Meanwhile sub-Saharan Africa's debt crisis has worsened. Its total debt stock has tripled to more than $180 billion since the early 1980s, which represents more than its aggregate national incomes. Repayments on that debt absorb $11 billion annually, or four times what African governments spend on health and welfare. Even this is only part of the story, since repayments are made at less than half of scheduled levels, so that arrears are accumulating at a frightening rate.

World Bank efforts to promote exports of coffee, cocoa and tea have achieved considerable success. The problem is that as more primary exporters seek their share of commodity markets, characterized by relatively fixed demand, prices have fallen to their lowest level in 90 years in real terms. This is why countries such as Ghana, Uganda and Ivory Coast increased their exports of coffee and cocoa by over half between 1985 and 1990, only to see foreign exchange earnings shrink because of falling prices. The vicious circle of an economic decline, in which sub-Saharan Africa is trapped, will only be broken if the IMF and the World Bank chart a new policy course. As the Asian 'tigers' have shown, recovery and poverty reduction need state intervention.

(Source: adapted from Kevin Watkins, 'A continent driven to economic suicide', *Guardian*, 20 July 1994.)

(a) Why does the author view international debt as a major problem for many developing countries in Africa? [*10 marks*]

(b) Using economic analysis, explain the problems associated with dependency on primary products faced by countries such as Ghana, Uganda and Ivory Coast. [*20 marks*]

(c) Critically examine the views that 'recovery and poverty reduction need state intervention'. [*20 marks*]

London

Question 2

(a) Why does the underlying rate of economic growth vary from one country to another? [*12 marks*]

(b) Discuss the difficulties which are likely to be faced by a poor developing country that aims to increase the rate at which its economy is growing. [*13 marks*]

AEB

Question 3

Is concern for the environment necessarily detrimental to economic growth and living standards?

UODLE

1 Solutions
Markets

1 (a) During the summer months, when strawberries are in season, supply is considerably greater than during the winter months when strawberries are imported. As supply increases, the price of strawberries falls and, in response, consumers expand their purchases. It is as simple as that!

(b) It is true that higher prices encourage production of most products, and strawberries are no exception to this rule. Decisions about strawberry production (like many other products) are made in advance of sales, but because of the growing time involved (it takes several years to create a mature field), these decisions are difficult to alter in response to price changes. The fall in price as the harvesting season gets under way is fully anticipated by producers, but if price falls below their expectations they will cut back on strawberry production in future years (the long run).

(c) Strawberries are highly perishable, and so, on any given day, the supply of strawberries to the shops and to the markets will be highly inelastic. However, it is possible for growers to vary the quantity of strawberries they pick. Thus we might expect the elasticity of supply of strawberries available directly from growers to be greater than the elasticity of supply in the shops or on the market.

2 (a) Traffic congestion on motorways could be reduced by introducing a system of tolls. This would encourage road users to find alternative routes which avoid the motorways and to share journeys or loads to a greater extent.

(b) It would be equally easy to eliminate road congestion in city centres by introducing a system of permits required to travel within the city centre. Permits could be sold by local authorities at prices high enough to discourage vehicle use in the city centre to the required level.

Question 1 – Student's answer

(a) There are several possible reasons why the price of coffee has increased. One reason involves the 'severe frost damage to Brazilian coffee plantations'. Brazil is easily the biggest supplier of coffee beans and the frost damage would therefore have a significant impact on world supply. As supply decreased, price would rise. We are also told that 'price had risen fivefold since January 1993; even before the Brazilian frost reports, the cost had been rising because some farmers, disheartened by low coffee prices worldwide, had moved on to more lucrative crops'. Again, as farmers cease production supply would decrease and price would rise. The effect of the reduction in supply is shown in Figure A1.1, where S_0 is the original supply curve and S_1 is the supply curve after the effect of the frost damage and the withdrawal of farmers from coffee production. D is the demand for coffee. As supply decreases (shifts to the left), the equilibrium price rises from P_0 to P_1 and the equilibrium quantity supplied and demanded falls from Q_0 to Q_1.

(b) The extract we are given implies that a cause of the price increase was the frost damage to crops in Brazil. However, this is unlikely to result in an immediate increase in the price of ground coffee in the shops. For example, the coffee beans must be

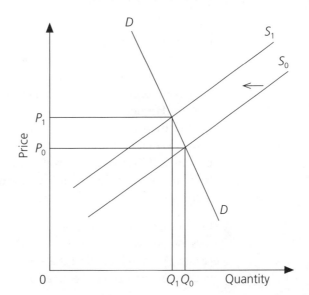

Figure A1.1 The effect of a reduction in supply on price

processed before they are available in the shops. Hence retailers may sell off their stocks at current prices and prices will only rise when stocks of coffee incorporating higher input costs are sold to consumers. Another reason might be that producers will prefer temporarily to absorb the rise in coffee prices by cutting their profit margins. However, sellers are unlikely to do this permanently, and so coffee prices will eventually rise.

(c) That the 'real cost of coffee has fallen more steeply' than the nominal price simply means that, after allowing for inflation, the cost of coffee has fallen even further than implied by the actual reduction in price.

(d) Cross-elasticity of demand measures the responsiveness of demand for one product to changes in the price of another product. Since tea and coffee are substitutes in consumption, the rise in the price of coffee in the 1970s 'encouraged a generation of students and young workers away from coffee and on to tea'.

(e) The International Coffee Agreement clearly regulated the price of coffee. To do this it must have been able to control the supply of coffee since it would not be able to control consumer demand. With the breakdown of the Agreement, supply is unregulated and so, in an attempt to increase their incomes, coffee growers have produced more and more coffee. This increase in supply then lowered prices. We are told that falling prices resulted in 'farmers turning to more lucrative crops'. The subsequent decrease in supply has forced up the price of coffee, which might encourage its production on a larger scale. In other words, coffee prices will become more unstable following the breakdown of the International Coffee Agreement.

Examiner's note A good answer which uses the data to answer the question

Question 2 – Outline answer

Section (a) is relatively straightforward, but it carries almost half the total marks available for the question. To score high marks you must ensure that you give thorough and detailed answers to each of the sub-sections. It is important to support your discussion with relevant examples and perhaps diagrams.

(a) (i) In a market economy, changes in **relative** prices give signals to producers and consumers. Changes in prices might signal to consumers the existence of surpluses or shortages. They also signal to producers that consumer preferences have changed. For example, when society demands more of a product, its price rises and resources are competed away from alternative uses as producers supply more of that product. A simple demand and supply diagram might help your explanation here.

(ii) Prices act as a means of rationing output among consumers. In this sense, the distribution of output to consumers is rather like an auction. Prices go on

rising until only those consumers willing **and able** to pay the higher price remain. As price rises, more and more consumers are forced out of the bidding (or drop out) and therefore have to make alternative purchases.
(iii) In a market economy, production is encouraged through the profit motive. Successful producers make higher profits. The market therefore rewards success. Higher relative prices – that is, a rise in the price of some goods relative to others – changes the profits available from producing different goods. When consumers demand more of one good, the price of that good increases. This raises the profits available from producing it and in this way provides an incentive to increase production of the good whose price has increased.

(b) Many arguments could be considered for section (b) and you should note that the question asks you to evaluate them: that is, make reasoned judgements about their validity. You might consider the arguments listed below, though not all of them would stand up to critical evaluation!

(b) *For*
   (i) Since school income would be dependent on attracting pupils, schools would have an incentive to meet the needs of pupils.
   (ii) It would provide an incentive for schools to improve their performance because it would enable them to charge higher fees.
   (iii) So long as the voucher had a high enough value, it would ensure that all pupils could obtain a satisfactory education.
   (iv) By introducing the concept of payment for education, pupils might be encouraged to increase the level of their efforts!
   (v) It might lead to a reduction in public expenditure.

Against
   (i) Because of inadequate information, parents and pupils might not make the optimum choice of school.
   (ii) Education is a merit good, and by introducing vouchers some of the positive externalities associated with education might be lost.
   (iii) Schools might be more likely to provide courses which are popular with parents but which are educationally more questionable.
   (iv) Because the most successful schools would be able to charge higher fees, the voucher system would remove equality of opportunity in education by denying pupils from poorer backgrounds the opportunity to attend schools which might better serve their needs.
   (v) Because of their inability to levy supplementary fees, schools in poorer areas might not obtain the level of funding necessary to provide proper educational provision for their pupils.

Question 3 – Outline answer

(a) To score well on this part of the question you need to define each of the concepts and to show how they can be measured. You could then discuss the implications of an inelastic PED: that is, where a change in price leads to a less than proportional change in quantity demanded. It is a good idea to give a little elaboration on each estimate, for example by noting that in this case each 1 per cent rise in price leads to a fall in quantity demanded of 0.8 per cent. In the case of income elasticity of demand, we find a positive value for all normal goods because as income rises, demand tends to rise. Again, it is useful to note that, in this case, a 1 per cent rise in income leads to a 2.8 per cent rise in demand. When cross-elasticity of demand is positive, the products are substitutes because a rise in the price of one product is associated with a rise in demand for the other. When cross-elasticity is negative, the products are complements because a rise in the price of one product is associated with a reduction in demand for the other. In this particular case the products are substitutes, so, for example, a 1 per cent rise in the price of cinema tickets might be associated with a 1.5 per cent rise in demand for video recordings. You might also comment on the fact that (i) refers to movement along the demand curve, and (ii) and (iii) refer to shifts in the demand curve.

(b) There are many areas that might be discussed here and it is important to show awareness of the implications of the different estimates of elasticity given in the question. One important point to explore is that these estimates, although assumed to be accurate at the time they were computed, are unlikely to be constant. The figures might be the result of being computed at a particular stage of the business cycle and the firm is therefore likely to interpret them with caution. Certainly the price inelastic demand for the product does imply that a rise in price will lead to an increase in total revenue, and the reduction in sales must reduce some costs. Profits (revenue – cost) are therefore likely to increase by raising price, but there may be limits to this price raising policy. For example some substitutes are available (e.g. cinemas) and this may restrict the scope for price increases, and the firm will clearly have to consider the possible reaction of rival suppliers. The magnitude of income elasticity does imply that future growth prospects are encouraging, since national and personal income will continue to grow in the long term. This has implications for the firm's investment policy, particularly in new outlets for its products.

2 Solutions
Market structure and private industry

SOLUTIONS TO REVISION ACTIVITIES

1 As long as the firm can at least cover its variable costs of production it is making some contribution to the fixed costs already incurred. However, in the long run it must cover all its costs, both fixed and variable. The fixed costs of production are therefore the maximum acceptable short-run loss. Any losses greater than this would imply that the firm is not even covering its short-run variable costs. It would then be better to leave the industry and avoid making its eventual loss even larger. In the long run the firm must cover all its costs including an element of normal profit.

2 To maximize profit, the firm must equate marginal cost with marginal revenue in each market. We know that marginal cost is £16, so by equating this with the marginal revenues in each market we can obtain the profit-maximizing price and sales in each market. Given that the firm produces 9 units, profit is maximized when: 4 units are sold in Market A at a price of £7 per unit; 3 units are sold in Market B at a price of £8 per unit; and 2 units are sold in Market C at a price of £9 per unit.

ANSWERS TO PRACTICE QUESTIONS

Question 1 – Student's answer

(a) In competitive oligopoly, firms face a kinked demand curve. They know that if they increase the price of their product, other firms will not retaliate. The firm which

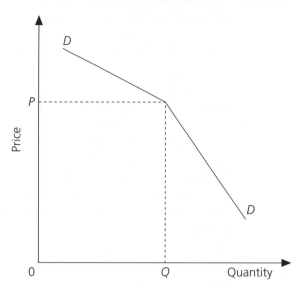

Figure A2.1 The kinked demand
curve in competitive oligopoly

increases price in a competitive oligopoly will therefore not lose many customers to rival firms. However, if a firm cuts its price there will be swift retaliation from other firms, otherwise they will lose customers to the price cutter. We can see this situation in Figure A2.1. If the firm raises its price, we can see that demand for its product is elastic because other firms will leave their price unchanged. However, if the firm lowers its price, demand for its product is inelastic because other firms will match the price cut. This is how firms behave in competitive oligopoly.

Examiner's note   Demand is not necessarily inelastic below the kink, it is simply less elastic than it is above the kink.

The situation is different in collusive oligopoly. Here firms cooperate to determine price and output: in other words, they form a cartel. This means that they operate as if they were a monopoly. They produce where marginal cost equals marginal revenue for the whole industry, and then give each individual firm a quota which that firm produces and sells. There is no competition between the firms. They just agree on what strategy to follow.

Examiner's note   This is quite a good answer. Good to see you have presented a diagram. However, the answer could have been developed a little further to make it even better. The MR curve and its discontinuity beneath the kink point (which could be labelled!) could be drawn and used to explain price rigidity.

(b) Big firms can gain economies of scale which lead to lower prices for the consumer. Because of this, it is desirable for firms to grow. However, if they grow too big they acquire monopoly power, which enables them to charge consumers higher prices than would exist if they did not have that power. The problem seems to be: how can we gain the advantages of large-scale production without paying higher prices?

If firms are free to enter and leave the industry, there are no barriers to entry or exit. This means that firms can enter and leave the industry until all earn normal profit. Monopolies rely on barriers to entry to enable them to charge high prices and so preserve their supernormal profit. However, when there are no barriers to entry, then there is nothing to stop firms from entering an industry and competing away any supernormal profit because competition will lead to lower prices.

Monopolies might not always earn supernormal profit. It is possible that they might only earn normal profit. The problem is that the amount of profit earned is not the only argument against monopoly. Another problem is that monopolies have no incentive to produce efficiently because there is no competition. Again, if there are no barriers to entry, any firm producing inefficiently will be noticed by other firms, who will then come into the industry if they can produce more efficiently than existing producers. Thus we see that there is no need for government intervention, because when there are no barriers to entry, efficiency is encouraged.

Examiner's note   Monopolies have a powerful incentive to improve efficiency since any extra profit earned is not competed away. However, this is quite good although the analysis could have been deepened and widened a little to bring in other problems associated with barriers to entry. You are talking about contestable market theory, so mention this term and consider its implication a little more thoroughly.

Question 2 – Outline answer

(a) It is best to begin with a definition of privatization, and then to outline the reasons why privatization has been a feature of government policy. One reason is to improve efficiency with which firms operate instead of underwriting losses, as happens in the case of loss-making industries in public ownership. There might be efficiency gains because industries are now run on commercial lines. The revenue from asset sales has also reduced the need for government borrowing, which might have aided control of the money supply without having to raise interest rates to the same extent. There are also political reasons for privatization. Creating a property-owning democracy has been an aim of the government.

(b) You will need to include some data to answer this part of the question. It would be useful to discuss how much had been raised through sales of assets, and how productivity per employee had changed in the post-privatization era. Note that there has been considerable criticism of equity having been sold at well below their true market value. You might also discuss the extent to which the privatized industries have responded to consumer demand. Their record has not always been good here – look at the number of complaints to the regulatory bodies!

Question 3 – Outline answer

It is best to begin with a brief statement defining what privatization implies, and then to discuss the possible advantages of state ownership of monopolistic industries compared with private ownership of monopolies.

In many privatization cases, the fact is that a state monopoly has been replaced by a private monopoly, but in more recent years the government has gone some way towards preventing this. For example, the privatization of the Central Electricity Generating Board was broken up and the generating business of the CEGB was split into three new businesses.

One advantage of public ownership of monopolies is the presumption that they will not exploit their position to earn supernormal profit. You can illustrate this with an appropriate diagram (see p. 22) but you must also discuss the regulations in place to prevent the abuse of monopoly power. They are also in a position to take account of externalities generated as a result of production and consumption, and so, by adjusting output accordingly, can achieve a more optimal allocation of resources. In particular, this might imply providing socially desirable, but uneconomic, services. Investment decisions in state-owned industries can be varied to boost demand in times of recession and curtail demand in times of boom.

However, these advantages might be lost if a monopoly is privatized, but other advantages might be gained. One problem with state ownership of monopoly is that there is no emphasis on improving efficiency. A privatized monopoly could gain greater profits by improved efficiency – efficiency which might be further improved by the absence of government interference in investment decisions. There are other points to consider which might imply that private ownership of monopoly is a success: for example, asset sales also increase government revenue and reduce the need for government borrowing, while there might be greater emphasis on product quality, meeting the needs of consumers, and so on.

3 Solutions
Market failure

1 When an individual is vaccinated against a contagious disease this benefits both the individual privately and society generally. If individuals had to pay for vaccinations, demand would be less than the optimal rate because individuals would not consider the benefits to society from having themselves vaccinated.

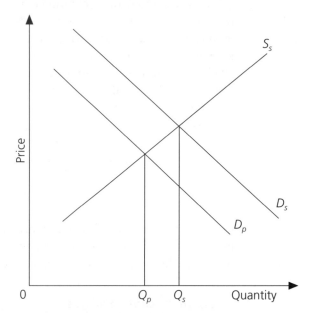

Figure A3.1 The demand for vaccinations is less when only private benefits are considered than when social benefits are considered

▶ In this case, the **marginal social benefit** from consumption diverges from the **marginal private benefit** (as reflected in the price the consumer pays for the last unit consumed).
▶ In Figure A3.1, D_p shows the demand for vaccinations when only the private benefits are considered and S_s shows the marginal social cost of providing vaccinations.
▶ The total number of vaccinations is Q_p.
▶ D_s represents the demand for vaccinations when the marginal social benefit is considered. Consumption of vaccinations now rises to Q_s.

2 If the marginal social cost of production is *less* than the marginal social benefit, then the allocation of resources can be improved by an increase in production – even if this involves an increase in pollution!

3 When goods are provided freely to consumers, the opportunity cost of consumption is zero and therefore the tendency will be to overconsume. The problem is to identify the optimal rate of consumption. (Note that the recent emphasis on reforming the NHS implies that there might be overconsumption of health care in relation to the optimum level.)

Question 1 – Student's answer

(a) Market failure arises when consumption of a particular good is above or below the socially optimum level: that is, marginal social benefit is not equal to marginal social cost.

Road congestion is an example of market failure because road users consider only marginal private benefit and the marginal private cost of using private transport. They do not consider that, by using cars instead of public transport, they cause

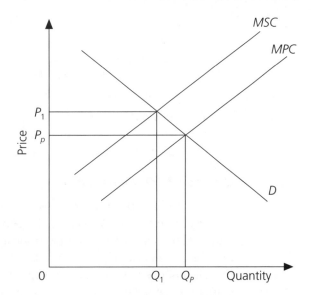

Figure A3.2 Price and quantity in relation to both marginal private costs and marginal social costs

congestion and delays. This is important because time is money and delays mean that time is wasted, so that productive activities are not taking place as efficiently as possible.

The reason why road congestion is an example of market failure can be seen by reference to Figure A3.2. Here we can see that demand for private motoring is downward sloping. As the cost of motoring falls, more people use private transport. MPC is the marginal private cost curve and includes the costs incurred by motorists when they use their own cars. MSC is the marginal social cost of motoring and includes the private marginal cost as well as the 'external' cost of road congestion. From the diagram we can see that the private cost of motoring is P_p and at this price consumption is equal to Q_p. However, if we consider the marginal social cost of motoring, the optimal price would be P_1 and consumption would be Q_1. Market failure is apparent in this example, because to achieve maximum efficient consumption of private motoring, it should fall by $Q_p - Q_1$.

Examiner's note An excellent, maturely written answer using many relevant concepts and ideas. A good diagram presented and well used in the answer.

(b) There are many policies a government might pursue to deal with the problem of road congestion. One solution is to charge road users for using roads. In the case of motorway traffic this is easy, and such roads could become toll roads. In towns, however, it is not so easy to introduce tolls. Indeed, attempts to do so might even increase congestion.

A different system might be to sell permits which allow road users to bring their cars into the city centre. Any road user who does not display some sort of certificate or disc indicating that they have paid to bring their vehicle into the city centre would be fined. This would increase the marginal private cost of private vehicle use so that it more closely accords with the marginal social cost of private motoring. Consumption would then fall towards the socially optimum rate.

A completely different approach is to increase the efficiency of public transport through more government investment. Consumption of public transport could also be increased if public transport was granted a subsidy, so that the price of public transport would fall compared with the cost of private transport.

Another solution is to restrict the availability of car parking spaces or else to increase the cost of parking in car parks. If it became more difficult for people to find parking spaces they would be compelled to use public transport. Alternatively, if the cost of parking in public car parks was increased, road users would again cut back on their use of private cars because of the additional expense involved.

Increasing the cost of private motoring seems to be the best way of dealing with market failure caused by congestion, and one obvious way of increasing the cost of motoring is to increase the tax on petrol and diesel. This means that those motorists who cover more miles pay higher costs than those who cover fewer miles. Here again, the increased cost of private motoring would lead to a reduction in consumption.

We have looked at several ways of dealing with the problem of road traffic congestion. None of them are perfect, but at least if the cost of motoring is increased, consumption will decline to nearer the socially optimum level.

Examiner's note   Very good. Many useful policies raised and discussed. Perhaps you could have used your earlier diagram or presented a new one to show how taxes might have helped obtain the social optimum road use.

Question 2 – Outline answer

(a) Clearly you must begin your answer to this part of the question by defining what externalities are. You could then go on to explain the distinction between marginal private cost and marginal social cost, indicating that pollution enters into the calculation of the latter but not the former. It would be useful to illustrate the effect of this diagrammatically and to show that, in a free market, the existence of a negative externality leads to consumption above the socially optimum rate.

(b) There are many policies that a government might use to deal with the problem of pollution. You are asked to **evaluate** and you should ensure that you are clear what this term implies. Pollution permits and taxing polluters are two possible solutions, and these are outlined on pp. 32–33.

Question 3 – Outline answer

(a) Externalities have been defined on p. 30, and at this stage you should know how to define them by heart!

(b) Whether the government should provide those goods which generate externalities depends on whether negative or positive externalities are generated. If they are negative, then it could be argued that production controlled by the state would ensure that production was restricted to the socially optimum rate. In the case of monopoly, it could be argued that state control of monopoly would reduce the emphasis on profit maximization and allow production to be expanded to the point at which marginal cost equals the price consumers are prepared to pay for the last unit they consume (see p. 34). In the cases of public goods and merit goods, state provision could ensure that the socially optimal amount is available to society. Each of these implies that the state knows the socially optimal rate of provision and would be willing to make that amount available to society. This might not be so. There are also implications for taxation and government expenditure which you need to explore. You might conclude that it would be impossible for a government to be the sole provider of every good which generates an externality, not least because this would be unacceptable to society. For example, traffic jams imply the existence of an externality, but nobody would seriously suggests that private ownership of cars should be banned!

4 Solutions
Inequality and poverty

SOLUTIONS TO REVISION ACTIVITIES

1 The higher earnings of males compared with females strongly suggests the existence of sex discrimination. However, the higher earnings of males might also be due to many other factors. Males tend to be more highly unionized than females, for example, and females are disproportionately represented in low-paid occupations such as catering.

2 Education is, of course, not the only factor influencing income. It is true that in developed economies education is freely available to all between certain ages and there is no inequality in the distribution of ability. There are also other factors to consider, such as incomes derived from wealth, type of work undertaken, and so on.

3 If the Gini coefficient is increasing, the distribution of income is becoming less even. The lowest value the Gini coefficient can take is zero when there is perfect equality in the distribution of income.

ANSWERS TO PRACTICE QUESTIONS

Question 1 – Student's answer

A trade union is an organization formed with the aim of collectively representing the views of its members in negotiations with their employer. The ability of a trade union to obtain pay rises depends on its ability to restrict the supply of labour. The greater the ability of the union to restrict the supply of labour, the greater its ability to obtain a pay rise. The extent of the pay rise the union can negotiate and the employment consequences of this pay rise are determined by several factors.

One particularly important factor is the elasticity of demand for labour by the employer. The more elastic the demand for labour, the lower the ability of a trade union to obtain a pay rise for its members and the greater the numbers who will become unemployed as a result of any pay rise. Figure A4.1 illustrates this point, where D_0 and D_1 show the demand curve for two different groups of workers who both obtain the same pay rise. It is clear that the same pay rise will have a greater impact on employment when demand is given by D_0 (the more elastic demand curve) than when demand is given by D_1. When demand is given by D_0, a wage increase of $W_0 W_{01}$ leads to a reduction in the number of workers employed of $N_0 N_{01}$. When demand is given by D_1, the same pay rise, shown as $W_1 W_{12}$, leads to a reduction in the number of workers employed of only $N_1 N_{12}$.

So what are the factors that influence the elasticity of demand for labour? A major determinant is the demand for the product which labour produces. If this is inelastic, the demand for labour will also tend to be inelastic. Another important determinant is the proportion of total costs represented by labour costs. If labour costs are a small proportion of total costs, the demand for labour will tend to be less elastic than otherwise, and so any given pay rise will have a lower impact on numbers employed. The ease with which capital can be substituted for labour is another important factor to consider. If capital is easily substituted for labour, any given pay rise will have a larger impact on employment than if it is difficult or expensive to substitute capital for labour.

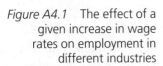

Figure A4.1 The effect of a given increase in wage rates on employment in different industries

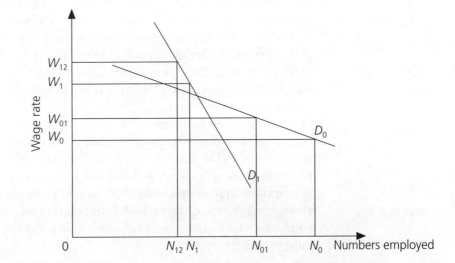

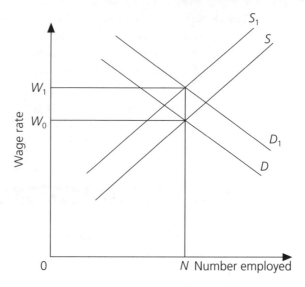

Figure A4.2   The effect of a wage increase financed entirely by an increase in productivity is to leave employment unchanged

If the trade union is able to negotiate a pay rise in return for increased productivity, it is possible that the increase in pay will have no effect on numbers employed. An increase in productivity implies that the average worker produces more, and, as a consequence, demand for labour will increase. A rise in pay, on the other hand, has the effect of reducing the supply of labour. As can be seen in Figure A4.2, the effect of an increase in wages from W_0 to W_1 is to leave employment unchanged at N. A similar situation would exist if demand for the product was rising and firms were able to pass on the effect of higher costs in the form of higher prices without loss of sales.

Other ways in which a trade union might be able to obtain a pay rise for its members is, first, if it is able to persuade employers to accept a cut in profits. Secondly, a pay rise is possible without redundancies if the recruitment of new staff is restricted. By ensuring that the supply of labour falls through natural wastage, those workers who remain in employment will be able to obtain a pay rise. Thus a pay increase has been obtained at the expense of numbers employed, although there have been no redundancies.

Examiner's note   Some excellent economic analysis here. Relevant diagrams have been presented and these are very well used in the text. Well written and clearly structured. This will achieve the highest grade.

Question 2 – Outline answer

(a) The answer to this part of the question is differences in the supply and demand conditions for the different types of skill. The demand for secretaries is likely to be more elastic that the demand for solicitors. A great deal of secretarial work can be undertaken without much training and, to this extent, there are more substitutes for the skills of a secretary than for the skills of a solicitor. Demand for secretaries will therefore be more elastic than demand for solicitors. On the supply side, it takes years of training to become a solicitor and requires a great deal of innate ability. Secretaries are more easily trained and, in general, require less innate ability. Because of these factors, the supply of solicitors will be lower and less elastic than the supply of secretaries. It would be useful to illustrate these points with an appropriate diagram.

(b) Wage differentials are important in allocating labour. Changes in the demand for certain goods and services motivate changes in the wage rates offered by different occupations, and to this extent, wage differentials are important in the allocation of resources. You must discuss this in full and illustrate your points with appropriate diagrams, showing how changes in supply and demand lead to changes in prices and wages. Link your points to mobility of labour and emphasize that higher wages encourage changes in the supply of labour to different occupations.

Question 3 – Outline answer

(a) Although you are not specifically asked to do so, it is best to begin your answer to this part of the question with a definition of poverty (see p. 39). You could then go on to discuss the impact of social security benefits on the distribution of income. These benefits are targeted specifically at those on lower incomes and have a marked impact on the distribution of income. However, there are problems, because increased spending on social security increases government expenditure, which might lead to higher interest rates and inflation as the money supply rises. Both of these effects will tend to have a greater impact on those on low incomes. Increased social security payments might also discourage some workers from seeking employment.

(b) Tax reductions benefit all tax payers, but particularly benefit those at the lower end of the earnings scale. By reducing the amount taken in taxation they might encourage more workers to seek employment. Again, lower taxes might leave the government with problems of increased borrowing.

(c) Subsidies on food, fuel and housing will benefit all consumers but, given that these goods account for a greater percentage of expenditure of lower-income groups than higher-income groups, they will have some impact on the extent of poverty. The problem with subsidies is that they adversely affect the allocation of resources, a point you should discuss in some detail.

5 Solutions
Inflation and unemployment

SOLUTIONS TO REVISION ACTIVITIES

1 If inflation is stable and predictable, its future value will be known. Hence the price mechanism will more accurately transmit information about changes in consumer preferences. Also, if inflation is stable and predictable, its future value can be taken into account when fixing prices and wages for the period ahead. It will therefore have less impact on the distribution of income. Despite this, it is important to realize that even if inflation is stable and predictable, this does not imply that it confers benefits on the economy or that it ceases to be a problem. For example, it might still cause problems in the balance of payments.

2 When there is an increase in the rate of money growth, economic agents must receive more money. An increase in the rate of money growth will therefore leave economic agents with excess money balances **at the existing price level**. Since they have more money than they desire to hold they will spend more. This implies that any increase in aggregate demand will pull prices upwards.

3 If velocity of circulation is constant, the demand for money is also constant. Velocity measures the average rate at which economic agents spend their money balances. A fall in velocity therefore implies that, on average, economic agents are holding money for longer periods: that is, the demand for money has increased.

4 When the rate of inflation is falling, the level of unemployment must be above the natural rate, and therefore the labour market is in disequilibrium.

ANSWERS TO PRACTICE QUESTIONS

Question 1 – Student's answer

In this essay I will use aggregate demand and aggregate supply analysis to compare the effect of cuts in income tax with reductions in unemployment benefits as a method of reducing unemployment.

Examiner's note   In general, avoid signposts like this.

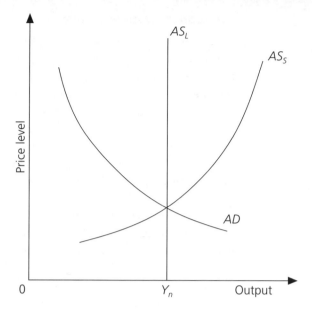

Figure A5.1 Aggregate
demand and aggregate
supply in the short run
and the long run

Aggregate demand is the total demand for goods and services in an economy. We can
write:

$AD = C + I + G + X - M$

where:

  AD = aggregate demand;
  C = consumption expenditure, by households;
  I = investment by firms;
  G = government expenditure;
  X = exports; and
  M = imports.

We know that demand varies inversely with market price, so aggregate demand curves
slope downwards from left to right as shown in Figure A5.1.

Examiner's note   It isn't obvious and you need to give some explanation.

Aggregate supply is also related to price. As price rises, firms are encouraged to
produce more and so supply rises with price. This implies that aggregate supply curves
slope upwards from left to right. However, this is only true in the short run. In the long
run, price has no influence on the decisions of firms about how much to produce, because
there is a natural rate of output. Figure A5.1 shows the way aggregate demand and
aggregate supply vary with price, and also the equilibrium level of output.

Examiner's note   A little more detail on the reasons for the behaviour of aggregate
supply would help. You should also explain how equilibrium is determined.

We can analyse the effect of a reduction in income tax on unemployment using the
aggregate demand and aggregate supply framework we have just explained. A reduction
in income tax will obviously increase disposable income. Because disposable income has
gone up, spending will go up, and this implies an increase in aggregate demand. Because
of this, output will go up and unemployment will go down. This happens because, as we can
see from Figure A5.1, output rises as the price rises. However, Figure A5.1 also shows
that in the long run, supply cannot increase above the natural rate, and so any reduction
in unemployment because of a reduction in income tax is only temporary.

Examiner's note   Give more detail to explain why unemployment goes down when
expenditure increases and why the reduction in unemployment is only temporary.

The same is not true of a reduction in unemployment benefit. If the government decides
to cut unemployment benefit, then obviously disposable income will go down and

unemployment will go up as aggregate demand falls. But in this case, the economy does not return to the natural rate. Instead, the increased hardship caused by a reduction in unemployment benefit causes unemployed people great hardship and they are compelled to accept low-paid jobs in order to survive. Because of this, a reduction in unemployment benefit will actually cause a reduction in unemployment.

Examiner's note   This is a good point and you might have elaborated on the determinants of the natural rate.

Examiner's note   Some very good analysis here. Aggregate demand and supply clearly defined at the start although not in as much detail as they might have been. Good diagram presented *but* it could have been *used* a little more in the text to illustrate your good points. In general the essay lacks development.

Question 2 – Outline answer

(a) To answer this question you need to demonstrate some familiarity with UK unemployment over the last decade. The level of unemployment is roughly the same, at 11 per cent, as it was a decade ago, but the composition of unemployment has changed. There are now more long-term unemployed workers than a decade ago and youth unemployment is also higher.

   In explaining the changes that have taken place you could consider the effect of such factors as the impact of exchange rate changes and changes in the rate of interest. Technological change has also had an effect. (Most estimates of the natural rate of unemployment suggest that it has increased over the last decade.) The impact of foreign competition on certain industries has been particularly important, and so on.

(b) You could begin your answer to this part of the question by stressing the points, first, that policy has been mainly directed at reducing the rate of inflation, and secondly, that the government does not really have a policy aimed at reducing unemployment! Nevertheless, you do also need to consider the effect of such policies as changes in fiscal policy, interest rates, exchange rate policies and supply-side policies. In the latter context, you might stress the impact of supply-side policies in relation to the operation of the labour market.

Question 3 – Outline answer

(a) (i) Clearly it is important to begin with a definition of the natural rate of unemployment as the rate that exists when the labour market is in equilibrium. This occurs when there is no tendency for inflation or unemployment to change. It would be useful to illustrate the natural rate of unemployment diagrammatically and to explain why it is the equilibrium rate of unemployment.

(ii) The magnitude of the natural rate depends on such factors as the skills the labour force possesses, the mobility of labour, whether a minimum wage exists, union restrictions on entry to certain occupations, the extent to which labour and product markets are free of regulations which restrict competition, rates of income tax and social security benefits, and so on. You must discuss the impact of these on the natural rate of unemployment.

(b) The natural rate hypothesis suggests that demand management policies have no effect on unemployment in the long run, and attempts to reduce unemployment below the natural rate by increases in aggregate demand will simply generate higher inflation. You must explain this in terms of the aggregate demand/ aggregate supply framework outlined on pp. 45–47. This explains the reliance on supply-side policies to combat unemployment and you must explain, again in terms of the aggregate demand/aggregate supply framework, how these policies are supposed to work.

Solutions
International issues

1 (a) Country A has an absolute advantage in the production of clothing since it requires fewer resources to produce one unit of clothing than country B.

(b) The opportunity cost of one unit of food in country A is 0.67 units of clothing. The opportunity cost of food in country B is 0.5 units of clothing. Country B therefore has a comparative advantage in the production of food.

2 (a) (i) Country A will obtain wheat from the cheapest source, and when it maintains a tariff of 4, country C is the cheapest source.

(ii) If country A sets a tariff of 6 against imports of wheat, it will grow its own wheat. (Cost of home produced wheat is 10. Cheapest imported source is country C at 11.)

(b) Countries A and B form a customs union. When A maintains a tariff of 6 against imports of wheat from outside the union, trade is **created** because wheat is imported from a cheaper source than domestic suppliers. However, if the tariff against imports of wheat from outside the union is set at 4, country A will switch from the low-cost supplier (country C) to a higher-cost supplier (country B). Trade is therefore **diverted** from the most efficient supplier to a less efficient supplier.

ANSWERS TO PRACTICE QUESTIONS

Question 1 – Student's answer

(a) (i) The initials GATT stand for the General Agreement on Tariffs and Trade.

(ii) Tariffs are a tax on imports and are therefore an overt barrier to trade. The common tariff against imports from outside the EU is an example of overt protectionism. Bogus health and safety standards are an example of covert protectionism. The European Court ruled that the UK ban on the import of turkeys, ostensibly to prevent the spread of 'Newcastle disease', was simply covert protectionism.

(iii) One reason why countries erect barriers to trade is to encourage the development of infant industries. These are industries which, if protected from foreign competition in the early stages of development, will grow, reap economies of scale and compete with established producers. Without protection, it is argued, such industries would fail to grow. A second reason for protection is the desire to prevent dumping. This occurs when one country exports its goods to another country at a cost below its real cost of production. The aim is obviously to eliminate competition so that a country becomes dependent on another country for supplies of a particular good.

Examiner's note   Good, succinct answers, well illustrated with examples.

(b) (i) The main advantage of free trade is that it encourages countries to specialize in producing those goods where they have greatest comparative advantage. The data does give some support for this view because it shows which countries are the biggest gainers from increased specialization encouraged by the operations of GATT.

Examiner's note   Good use of the data made here.

(ii) Two trading areas which have an advantage in textile production are Eastern Europe and the US. We are told that Eastern Europe is expected to gain $37bn annually from liberalization of trade in textiles and services: the gain to the service sector is estimated at $13bn, implying a gain to textiles of some $24bn. The data also tells us that the gain to the US in textiles from trade liberalization is $21.6bn. One important reason the US and Eastern Europe have an advantage in the production of textiles is that they have a climate suitable for textile production; not all countries have a climate suited to the production of textiles. Another important source of the advantage that these regions have in textile production is the relatively low wages paid to textile workers.

(iii) The gain to the US from trade liberalization is estimated at $36.4bn. Now if this is given a value of 100, the gains to the other regions can be measured as a percentage of the gain to the US. Thus:

▶ The gain to Asia, Asian Tigers, China and India is $67.5bn, which has an index value of 185.4.

▶ The gain to South America is estimated at $8bn, which has an index value of 22.0.

▶ There seems to be a problem with the data we are given because the bar chart shows a gain to Eastern Europe of $21bn, whereas the information under the diagrams indicates that the gain to Eastern Europe is $37bn. Taking 37bn as the correct figure, the gain to Eastern Europe and the EU is estimated at $98.3bn which has an index value of 270.

Examiner's note Very good. You have made it perfectly clear what you are doing.

(iv) The gain from GATT was much greater for the developed countries than for the developing countries. The top three developed countries/regions – the EU, the US and Japan – have a total gain of $124.7bn, compared with a total gain to the remaining developing countries of $89.9.

Examiner's note Data in part (i) could have been *used* a little more by way of illustration. Part (ii) is quite good, as is part (iii) though the *method* used to construct the index could have been made a little clearer.

(c) (i) ▶ When barriers to trade are dismantled, some industries decline because they can no longer compete with cheaper imports. The structure of demand changes and it is necessary for production to adjust in response. This is what is meant by the term 'structural adjustment of economies'.

▶ Sometimes externalities are generated as a result of production. One example of an externality is pollution, when producers dump their untreated waste into the environment. If producers were forced to clean up their waste materials before disposing of them, the cost of pollution would be internalized. Instead, society bears the cost as an externality.

(ii) One externality is an increase in unemployment as traditional industries decline. Another external cost that might arise as a result of structural adjustment is higher inflation if government borrowing is increased due to increased expenditure and reduced tax revenues following higher unemployment. A third externality is higher interest rates if these are increased to reduce downward pressure on the exchange rate because of an increase in imports.

Examiner's note A good, well expressed answer for these parts.

Question 2 – Outline answer

(a) One way to begin your answer to this question is to explain what is meant by the single market and its implications. The single market allows the free movement of goods and resources (labour and capital) between different countries. You could then briefly outline how the exchange rate mechanism operates. You might then discuss the extent to which certain aggregates such as inflation, government borrowing, interest rates and unemployment are converging. Common policies have also been established: for example, the CAP. There is also a European regional policy, monopolies and mergers policy, and so on.

(b) The economic issues are wide ranging but mainly focus on the likelihood of monetary union. Whether it is in the interests of particular countries such as the UK to be part of a monetary union is a matter of judgement, but the factors to be considered are those outlined above on pp. 55–56.

Question 3 – Outline answer

(a) A free floating exchange rate exists when exchange rates are determined by the free play of market forces. A fixed exchange rate is administered by the authorities and they intervene by buying and selling currency and adjusting the domestic rate of interest so as to preserve the fixed exchange rate.

(b) The exchange rate mechanism was a system of fixed exchange rates which were allowed to diverge from the 'central limit' within a margin of fluctuation. It was not a system of rigidly fixed exchange rates since intervention was only necessary after a currency diverged from its central limit by a specified amount.

Nevertheless, the ERM was ultimately a fixed rate system and any system of fixed exchange rates imposes limits on the conduct of domestic policy. By the time the UK withdrew from the ERM in September 1992, interest rates had been increased to preserve the exchange rate, but the effect of higher interest rates and what was widely considered to be an overvalued exchange rate was to throw the UK economy into quite severe recession. Since leaving the ERM, sterling at first depreciated rapidly as interest rates fell and the economy moved out of recession.

To score well on this section you must discuss the ways in which interest rates, the exchange rate and the state of the economy are related.

(c) This is the so-called j-curve effect. You could illustrate this diagrammatically and explain the reasoning behind the diagram, as explained on p. 55.

7 Solutions
Domestic economic policy: aims and instruments

SOLUTIONS TO REVISION ACTIVITIES

1 If the PSBR has a fixed target value this implies that policy is not used in a counter-cyclical way. As the economy moves into recession income falls. If policy is counter-cyclical, the PSBR should be increased as the government cuts taxes and increases its own expenditures. The opposite would happen in the boom phase of the cycle. A fixed target for the PSBR is therefore inconsistent with a counter-cyclical approach to economic policy.

2 A large and unexpected increase in the central government's budget deficit will almost certainly drive up interest rates. As government borrowing increases, the government will issue more securities and we might therefore expect security prices to fall. There is an inverse relationship between security prices and interest rates, and so, as security prices rise, interest rates will fall. This is easily demonstrated. Consider a bond with no redemption date which has a nominal value of £100 and which pays an annual rate of interest of 5 per cent. Suppose the bond is currently trading at £80; the rate of interest received by the holder of the bond is therefore $[(£5/£80)](100) = 6.25\%$.

3 GDP measures the amount produced by resources located in the UK economy regardless of the ownership of those resources. GNP measures incomes derived from the ownership of resources regardless of where they are located. Better estimates of changes in productivity can therefore be derived from changes in GDP since this measures changes in output from domestically based resources.

ANSWERS TO PRACTICE QUESTIONS

Question 1 – Student's answer

(a) (i) Nominal GNP is the market value of total income in a particular year. It can therefore change as a result of: a fluctuation in the rate of output; net property income from abroad; or inflation. However, it is fluctuations in output that are the main determinant of changes in unemployment. Because of this, there is a loose connection between nominal GNP and unemployment.

(ii) The connection between real GNP and unemployment is much more obvious and, in general, when real GNP rises at a faster rate, unemployment falls. Sometimes both occur in the same year, while at other times unemployment changes in the year following a change in real income.

Examiner's note Analysis is okay but you should illustrate with more reference to the data.

(b) Real GNP provides a better insight into changes in unemployment because, as explained above, changes in real GNP imply a change in the volume of production. A change in nominal GNP does not always reflect this. For example, in 1991 and 1992, real GNP fell but nominal GNP rose. We can see that in the same years unemployment rose.

Examiner's note Quite good. You have made better use of the data.

(c) (i) The PSBR is total borrowing in a particular year by the public sector, and the main determinant of this is the state of the central government's budget. Because of this, as economic activity rises, the PSBR will tend to fall, and when economic activity falls, the PSBR will tend to rise. For example, when economic activity is rising, tax revenues will be rising, and government expenditure on transfer payments will fall as unemployment falls and incomes rise.

(ii) The data support this view because we can see that, in general, when real GNP is rising, the PSBR is falling. Again in 1991 and 1992, when real GNP fell, the PSBR rose, yet in the previous years when real GNP rose, the PSBR fell. Unfortunately, the data is not conclusive because real GNP rose in 1993 and 1994, but the PSBR also went on rising.

Examiner's note On the right track, but a little more depth would help in part (i). Use of data in part (ii) is good as far as it goes, but more could have been made of *other columns* in the table. Notice that well over half of the total marks are available in this section so it is worth giving this section a little more attention.

(d) One factor that contributes to the magnitude of the PSBR is the extent of privatization: that is, the sale of public sector assets to the private sector. If assets are sold to the private sector, the revenue gained reduces the extent to which the rest of the public sector must borrow to finance its expenditure. In the longer term, the size of the PSBR is affected by the scale of privatization because many of the former nationalized industries were substantial loss-makers and these losses were financed by the state, which contributed to the PSBR. After privatization this burden disappears, and so the PSBR falls compared to the level that would have otherwise existed.

Examiner's note A good point.

Question 2 – Outline answer

(a) A whole host of factors could be discussed in the first part of this question. The rate of interest is determined by the supply and demand for money. Hence, in the long term, the most obvious way in which a government can influence the rate of interest is by restricting the rate at which the money supply grows. A more direct method is for the Bank of England to carry out an open-market sale of securities on a scale that will leave the money market short of funds. When the discount houses are compelled to borrow from the Bank, the Bank can lend at a rate *above* existing market rates. In consequence, the discount houses will raise their discount rates, and there will be a ripple effect that will spread throughout the money market and interest rates will rise. On the other side of the coin, the ability of the authorities to influence interest rates also depends partly on the behaviour of the PSBR. When this is rising, the government will be forced to increase its sales of debt, and as the price of bonds falls, interest rates will be forced upwards. The influence of the authorities also depends on the exchange rate regime. If the government has an exchange rate target, it must relinquish control of the rate of interest since it will be necessary to vary this in order to preserve the value of the exchange rate.

(b) In the long term, a rise in the rate of interest would tend to curtail the rate of growth of the money supply and, as predicted by the quantity theory of money, this would imply a fall in the rate of inflation. You could elaborate on the point by showing the effect of a significant rise in interest rates on aggregate demand. As aggregate demand falls, so the rate of inflation will tend to fall. To some extent, the impact of a rise in interest rates on the rate of inflation again depends on the exchange rate regime. If exchange rates were floating, then the impact on aggregate demand of a rise in interest rates would be reinforced because, if all other things remain equal, a rise in interest rates would tend to drive up the exchange rate. This would tend to reduce demand for exports (because the foreign price rises) and increase demand for imports (because the domestic price falls). To the extent that imports are a component of the RPI, or, in the longer term, to the extent that raw materials are imported, there would be further downward pressure on domestic inflation. If the exchange rate is fixed, then the domestic rate of inflation is heavily influenced by international rates of inflation.

   You must also discuss the fact that, in the short run, any rise in interest rates will affect the mortgage rate and, since this is a component of the RPI, inflation will rise.

Question 3 – Outline answer

(a) The rate of interest is simply the return to investors who lend funds, or the price that borrowers pay to obtain funds which must be repaid at some future date. There are many different types of interest rates in order to allow for loans of different duration and differences in the degree of risk associated with different loans. The nominal rate is simply the rate quoted to lenders and borrowers, and is the rate used to calculate the actual sum that must be paid over and above the amount borrowed. The simplest explanation of the real rate is that it is the nominal rate minus the rate of inflation.

(b) The point to stress here is that a rise in interest rates reduces aggregate demand as investment and demand for consumer durables fall. You can illustrate the effect on the equilibrium level of income either by using the 'Keynesian cross' diagram or by showing that, as aggregate demand falls, a short-run equilibrium level of income is established before income returns to the natural rate (see pp. 45–47).

(c) The main point to stress here is that if a central bank is independent, it is free to set its own monetary policy without interference from the government. A government might vary monetary policy in order to court short-run popularity at the expense of long-run goals. In particular, it might vary the rate of interest to stimulate aggregate demand in times of recession. However, in the longer term, the effect of this is simply to stimulate inflation because of the effect of lower interest rates on the money supply and aggregate demand. This cannot happen if interest rates are under the control of an independent central bank. The implication is that control of inflation is more assured if interest rates are controlled by an independent central bank. However, there is an additional consideration. If interest rates are controlled by an independent central bank, its statements on the future behaviour of the money supply will be more credible than statements by a government. This will reduce the unemployment cost of constraining inflation, because those who fix wages and prices will know in advance what the money supply will be.

8 Solutions
Economic growth and development

SOLUTIONS TO REVISION ACTIVITIES

1 Capital equipment, such as machinery, is many times more productive than labour. Capital does not require rest breaks or vacations and so on. Substituting capital for labour and utilizing the latest technologies has a profound impact on economic growth.

2 Primary products have not undergone any finishing to transform them in any way. In general, they are extracted from the earth or harvested. Such products tend to have a low price elasticity of demand so that changes in supply – for example, because of climatic changes in the case of agriculture – cause fluctuations in prices and therefore in the incomes of producers.

3 Poverty in the world's poorer countries has profound implications for the richer countries. If the poorer countries grow, the export potential for the richer countries will be vast as new markets for their products open up. In addition, poverty is often associated with instability and conflict. To the extent that conflicts spread, the richer countries might be drawn in. As a consequence, the richer countries might devote more resources to defence than otherwise, and the opportunity cost of this is likely to be a lower level of consumption than would otherwise be possible.

ANSWERS TO PRACTICE QUESTIONS

Question 1 – Student's answer

(a) Debt is viewed as a problem for sub-Saharan African countries because it has 'tripled to more than $180 billion since the early 1980s, which represents more than its aggregate national incomes'. We are told that repayments on this debt amount to $11 billion annually, which is four times greater than the amount these countries spend on health and welfare. Such levels of repayment would not be a problem if income was rising at a fast enough rate to enable these countries to meet their debt obligations with relative ease. However, this is clearly not the case since we are told that around 60 per cent of World Bank projects (financed by loans) 'fail to generate an economic return'. Furthermore, we are told that living standards have fallen by 2 per cent and continue to fall annually.

Examiner's note   A good answer, with selective and relevant use of the material presented.

(b) *Ghana, Uganda and Ivory Coast increased their exports of coffee and cocoa between 1985 and 1990 but prices fell by half (possibly as a result of increased supply), which reduced their foreign exchange earnings. The demand for primary products in general is price inelastic because of the lack of substitutes. In the short run, supply of primary products also tends to be inelastic. For example, the supply of coffee and cocoa depends on the size of the crop and this depends on the number of mature trees and on the weather. As supply has increased between 1985 and 1990, it is hardly surprising that price has fallen.*

Examiner's note   Some reasonable points but this is too brief, especially since it is worth 20 of the 50 marks in total. You could have presented and discussed a simple demand/supply diagram here.

(c) *The case for state intervention to promote economic recovery and poverty reduction is encouraged by its apparent success in the case of the Asian Tigers. The implication is that it has worked for these countries and therefore it will work for sub-Saharan Africa.*

One reason why the Asian Tigers have been successful is that they have invested heavily in education and have actively encouraged export-led growth. This approach might not be transferable to sub-Saharan Africa. The passage does not explicitly mention education but it does tell us that living standards are falling by 2 per cent a year. The implication is that health and welfare spending are relatively low. It is therefore reasonable to assume that spending on education is also relatively low.

While it might not be possible to replicate the success of the Asian Tigers by emphasizing the same policies, this does not necessarily imply that recovery and poverty reduction do not require state intervention. It might be possible to reform the fiscal system, thus developing incentives, particularly risk-taking, in order to encourage entrepreneurial talent.

Examiner's note   Quite good, but again this could be taken a *little* further.

Question 2 – Outline answer

(a) There are many reasons why the rate of economic growth would vary from one country to another. To answer this question you will need to discuss the importance of the different factors that promote growth. In modern economies, the rate of capital accumulation and technological progress are important, and hence you must consider the factors that promote both of these aspects, including: the extent of competition; the extent to which the banking sector and capital markets are developed; taxation and incentives; the extent to which the infrastructure is developed; the degree to which the labour force is educated and trained; and the resource endowments of the economy. With respect to the last point, remember that Russia is vastly richer than the USA in terms of its natural resource endowments, but that these resources are not exploited as efficiently in Russia as in the USA. The determinants of the savings ratio (the ratio of savings to income) are also important, because investment is impossible without savings.

(b) While it is true to say that countries differ, many of the poorer Third World countries do have certain common characteristics, including: a poorly developed infrastructure; reliance on subsistence agriculture with its low productivity; a poorly developed financial structure; a high rate of population growth; high debt obligations; and an inability to generate savings because of the necessity to devote resources simply to meeting basic needs. Many poorer countries also have climatic disadvantages, are riddled with corruption, and place social and religious restrictions on certain activities or on the participation of certain groups in the labour force. In most of these countries, investment in human capital is relatively low and illiteracy is common, while many of their products face restrictions on international markets, and so on. In general, you will earn higher marks if you can illustrate your points with examples.

Question 3 – Outline answer

One way to begin your answer to this question is by defining economic growth and by establishing the connection between economic growth and the environment through emphasis on the point that greater output usually requires greater resource input. You could illustrate this by showing an outward movement of a production possibility curve. When living standards are measured by per capita income, the standard of living rises whenever growth of output exceeds population growth. You might then go on to consider some detrimental environmental effects of increased production, such as degradation of the land and increased pollution and why, because of these externalities, changes in per capita income might not accurately reflect changes in the standard of living. You could then discuss the view that an optimum allocation of resources requires production to be pushed to the level at which marginal social benefit exactly equals marginal social cost. To this extent, concern for the environment is not inconsistent with economic growth. Additionally, it is also true that as output rises, the resources available to deal with environmental damage increase, and so economic growth might actually improve the environment!

Timed practice paper 1

This paper should be completed in 3 hours.

Question 1

(a) Distinguish between 'elastic supply' and 'inelastic supply'. [*20 marks*]
(b) Explain why the short-run supply of freshly cut flowers is likely to be less elastic than the supply of video recorders. [*40 marks*]
(c) Contrast the effect on price of a sudden increase in demand for both of these products. [*40 marks*]

London

Question 2

Table TP1   National newspaper circulation in the UK

Title of newspaper	Owned by	Daily circulation		
		1992	*1993*	*1994*
Sun	News Corporation	3,588,077	3,513,591	4,007,520
Daily Mirror	Headlington Investment	2,868,263	2,676,015	2,484,436
Daily Mail	Daily Mail	1,668,808	1,769,253	1,784,030
Daily Express	United Newspapers	1,537,726	1,490,323	1,369,266
Daily Telegraph	Ravelstone Corporation	1,043,703	1,024,340	1,007,944
Daily Star	United Newspapers	808,486	773,908	746,412
Today	News Corporation	495,405	533,332	579,910
Guardian	Guardian Newspapers	418,026	416,207	400,399
Times	News Corporation	390,323	368,219	471,847
Independent	Newspaper Publishing	376,532	348,692	284,440
Financial Times	Pearson	291,915	290,139	296,984
		13,507,264	13,204,019	13,433,188

Table TP2   UK newspaper price changes

	Old price (p)	New price (p)
Sun	25	20
Times	45	20
Telegraph	48	30

Note: The prices were reduced in early 1993.

(a) With reference to Table TP1, comment on the view that the News Corporation was a monopoly in the market for national daily newspapers in 1994. [*3 marks*]
(b) Suggest *two* reasons why some newspaper companies publish more than one newspaper title. [*4 marks*]
(c) Some of the other newspaper publishers considered that the price reductions announced by News Corporation for the *Sun* and *The Times* were an example of predatory pricing.
  (i) Explain what is meant by 'predatory pricing'. [*3 marks*]
  (ii) Examine *three* reasons which might explain why News Corporation embarked on such a pricing policy. [*6 marks*]

(d) To what extent might newspaper publishing be regarded as a contestable market? [*5 marks*]

(e) In the UK, newspaper publishers are prevented from controlling domestic independent television companies. Why might newspaper publishers seek to expand into other media? [*4 marks*]

London

Question 3

The data below is an adaptation of an article published in the *Financial Times* on 29 March 1993. Study the data carefully, then answer *each* of the questions which follow.

Pollution rights go to auction

The US government's Environmental Protection Agency (EPA) has introduced 'pollution permits' (pollution quotas) as part of its market-based strategy to reduce external costs of acid rain. One of the chief causes is the emission of sulphur dioxide (SO_2) into the atmosphere from chimneys.

The EPA has given emission permits to 110 SO_2 polluters, mainly electricity generation companies which use high-sulphur coal. Each permit is a quota which allows the company to emit 1 ton of SO_2 each year. The aim is to halve SO_2 emissions by the year 2000.

The programme works by allowing market supply and demand to encourage coal burners to cut SO_2 pollution. A firm which reduces its emissions below its quota will be able to sell the rest of the quota to another firm. It is hoped that this will encourage firms to invest in production technology and processes which will reduce SO_2 pollution (such as chimney 'scrubbers' and switching to gas or low-sulphur coal as a fuel). In the opposite case, a firm which exceeds its quota will have to cut production or buy excess permits from environmentally friendly companies.

At first, most of the permits are being given away free by the government. Later, the number of permits will be reduced each year and companies will have to bid for them at auction, paying the appropriate price to the EPA. It is expected that the price will rise, making investment by firms in emission-reduction more worthwhile. The US government believes that this will be a fairer and more cost-effective system of control than the present system of inspection and direct control by government orders. This involves government inspectors visiting industrial premises and their surroundings and giving orders to firms to reduce pollution (leading to fines when firms do not avoid or clean up pollution).

(a) Explain why acid rain might be regarded as an external cost. [*4 marks*]

(b) How would a pollution tax on firms which cause acid rain affect the market for a good or service? [*4 marks*]

(c) Using demand and supply theory, explain why the price of pollution permits is expected to rise each year. [*6 marks*]

(d) A sulphur emitting firm is considering whether to change its production processes in order to reduce its sulphur emissions. What factors would it take into account when making this decision? [*5 marks*]

(e) Explain the argument that compared to the present system of pollution control, pollution permits will be fairer and more cost-effective for the US government. [*6 marks*]

WJEC

Question 4
In 1992, average male earnings in the UK were £295.90 per week, whereas the average female earnings were £211.30 per week. How might this difference in male and female earnings be explained?

London

Timed practice paper 2

This paper should be completed in 3 hours.

Question 1

Pay rises: the dragon that can be slain

Ask ten economists for the most damaging cause of Britain's long-term economic performance and you will get different answers. High on the list, however, would be the question of how wages will change over the next twelve months.

Wages have been the economy's major problem for many years (see Figure TP1). All governments, especially in times of higher inflation, have asked workers to restrain their wage demands by accepting lower wage rises. When workers have ignored these requests governments have imposed maximum limits on pay rises, especially for their own employees.

Some commentators argue that pay rises cause no significant problem if they are equal to any increase in labour productivity. Others argue that this ignores the importance of the way in which UK wages compare with the levels paid by international competitors.

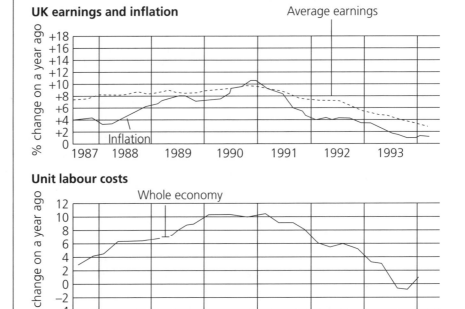

Figure TP1   Pay rises: the dragon that can be slain

(a) (i) Describe the changes in average earnings and inflation between 1987 and 1993. [*2 marks*]
    (ii) What do these changes suggest about what happened to living standards between 1987 and 1993? [*3 marks*]
(b) Using the data, explain the possible connection between wage rises and:

(i) unit labour costs; [*6 marks*]

(ii) inflation. [*6 marks*]

(c) Suggest and explain *two* problems which might be caused by government restrictions upon wage rises. [*4 marks*]

(d) Explain why wage rises are significant to the competitiveness of UK goods and services. [*4 marks*]

WJEC

Question 2

(a) Explain how changes in the external value of the pound (the exchange rate) affect the volume *and* value of UK exports. [*12 marks*]

(b) Discuss other factors which influence the sales of UK products in overseas markets. [*13 marks*]

AEB

Question 3

(a) Explain why 'broad' and 'narrow' measures of money are used. [*7 marks*]

(b) How might an increase in the money supply affect the level of prices, output and employment in an economy? [*18 marks*]

WJEC

Question 4

How useful are National Income statistics in comparing the standard of living in the UK with that in other countries?

WJEC

ANSWERS TO TIMED PRACTICE PAPER 1

Question 1

(a) Elasticity is a measure of responsiveness; in particular, elasticity of supply measures the responsiveness of quantity supplied to changes in price. It can be measured in the following way:

$$E_S = (\Delta Q/Q)(P/\Delta P)$$

where:

ΔQ = change in quantity supplied after the change in price;
Q = original quantity supplied before the change in price;
ΔP = change in price; and
P = original price.

So, for example, if the price of a product rises from £8.00 to £10.00 and, as a result, quantity supplied expands from 150 units per period to 200 units per period, elasticity of supply

$= (50/150)(8/2)$
$= 1.33.$

If elasticity of supply is greater than 1, supply is said to be elastic; if it is less than 1, supply is said to be inelastic; and if it equals 1, supply is said to be unitary. These three extreme possibilities are illustrated in Figure TP2.

(b) A major factor in determining the elasticity of supply of any product is the extent to which the product can be stored without deterioration and the cost of that storage. In the case of freshly cut flowers, storage is difficult and flowers must be

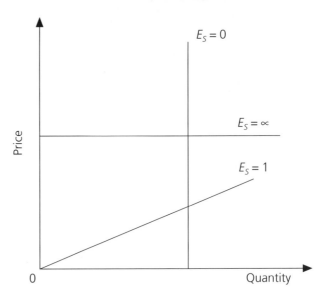

Figure TP2   Elasticity of
supply: the limiting cases

picked when they are ready. Once picked, they last only a short while. The same
is not, of course, true of video recorders. Once produced, they are easily stored
and the cost of storage is small in relation to the selling price of the product. This
alone would ensure that the elasticity of supply of video recorders was more elastic
than that of freshly cut flowers, but there are other factors that also explain the
more elastic supply of video recorders.

Freshly cut flowers are often grown locally and are relatively expensive to
transport in relation to their selling price. Any increase in price would therefore
draw on local supplies The same is not true of video recorders.

In the short run, the amount produced of any product can be increased by
working the variable factors more intensively with a fixed quantity of other
factors. The ease with which production can be increased is therefore an
important factor in determining the elasticity of supply in the short run. In the
case of video recorders, it would be possible to expand the production relatively
easily by purchasing more inputs and introducing overtime working to increase
production. The constraint here is likely to be the supply of component parts, but,
since these are easy and cheap to store, it is unlikely that this would be a problem.
It would also be relatively easy to cut back on production by introducing short-
time working.

Of course, if conditions permit, it is even easier to increase the quantity of
flowers available, since these can be picked by unskilled workers. However, a
major determinant of the amount of blooms ready to be picked is the weather
and, no matter how far the price of flowers rises, if weather conditions are
unfavourable, quantity supplied will be unresponsive to changes in price. When
flowers are ready to be picked, they must be picked within a relatively short space
of time. Even if price falls, so long as growers can cover the direct costs of supply
(labour, transport, etc.), much the same quantity will be supplied as would be the
case if the price of freshly cut flowers increased.

(c) The supply curve for both fresh flowers and video recorders will be upward
sloping with respect to price. Any increase in demand for either of these products
will therefore result in a rise in price. However, because the supply of fresh flowers
is likely to be less elastic than the supply of video recorders, a **given** increase in
demand for both products will result in a **proportionately greater** rise in the
price of fresh flowers. This is illustrated in Figure TP3, which shows the impact of
a 20 per cent rise in demand: that is, demand at each and every price increases by
20 per cent for both products.

In Figure TP3(a), D_f and S_f show the initial demand and supply for fresh flowers
while in Figure TP3(b), D_v and S_v show the initial demand and supply for video
recorders. D_{f1} and D_{v1} show where the respective demand curves for these

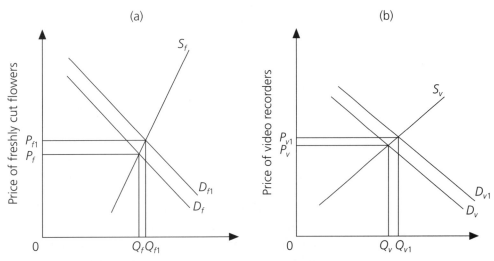

Figure TP3 The effect of a given change in demand on the price of a product depends on the ratio of elasticity of demand to elasticity of supply for the product

products would lie if demand for each increases by 20 per cent. In this case, it is clear that the increase in demand for fresh flowers causes a **proportionately** larger increase in the price of fresh flowers than the increase in demand for video recorders.

In fact, the effect of any change in demand for a product on the price of that product depends on its elasticity of demand and its elasticity of supply. In our example, elasticity conditions are such that differences in the elasticity of supply cause the increase in demand to have a different impact in each market. As explained above, video recorders are easily stored and there is a considerable range of different brands available. An inability on the part of consumers to obtain the particular video recorder that is their first preference leaves alternative sources of supply readily available. The availability of many different brands of video recorder again increases the elasticity of supply of such equipment, whereas there are few alternatives to fresh flowers, and an inability to obtain the desired product therefore implies that an increase in demand will drive prices steeply upwards.

Question 2

(a) Strictly, a monopoly is the sole supplier of a product. In this sense, no single supplier of newspapers is a monopoly. However, the legal definition of a monopoly is when a single firm supplies at least 25 per cent of the market. It is clear from the data we are given that News Corporation satisfies the legal definition of a monopoly since its three newspapers (*Sun, Today* and *The Times*) together account for over 37 per cent of the total newspaper market.

(b) There are many reasons why newspaper companies might wish to publish more than one newspaper title. Perhaps the most obvious reason is that different newspapers appeal to different consumers. The market does not consist of homogenous individuals, and different newspaper titles cater for the requirements of different readers. Note that different newspapers also sell at different prices indicating that consumers have different price elasticities of demand!

Another reason firms might prefer to have more than one newspaper title is that this enables them to increase their market share and spread their risks. If demand for one particular newspaper title declines then, to some extent, this decline can be absorbed because of sales of other newspaper titles. If a firm sells only a single newspaper title, any decline in sales might potentially result in closure of the firm.

(c) (i) Predatory pricing is an attempt by one firm to drive rival firms out of business by undercutting the prices offered by rivals. To do this the predator is prepared to charge a price less than that necessary to cover its total costs of production: that is, predatory pricing implies a willingness on the part of the predator to accept a short-run loss.

(ii) We can see from the data that newspaper publishing is not a growing market, and therefore News Corporation may have feared that the market would decline (it did decline in 1994 compared with its 1992 level) because of greater competition from other media such as television. It is also possible that News Corporation perceived demand for its product to be more price elastic than previously thought. The data we are given in Table TP1 indicates that daily sales of *The Times* and the *Sun* rose after these papers were reduced in price.

A third reason for the price policy is that News Corporation might simply have felt able to cross-subsidize from its other business interests any losses incurred as a result of its newspapers' price reductions.

(d) A contestable market exists when there are no barriers to prevent competitors entering the industry and nothing to prevent them leaving if profits do not match their expectations. This implies that there is no risk associated with undertaking production. Firms in the industry therefore have no market power, as in perfect competition, but the number of firms does not have to be large to generate this result.

To some extent the market might appear more contestable than several years ago. Changes in technology have made direct inputting of copy possible and this has profoundly reduced the fixed costs of newspaper production. In addition, the power of the print unions has diminished, so that they are no longer able to restrict the entry of new producers into the industry. The relatively recent emergence of *Today* and the *Independent* to some extent provides evidence of ease of entry.

On the other hand, there are entry and exit costs for a new firm coming into or leaving the industry. There are set-up and distribution costs of entry and, since the market is not expanding, any firm leaving the industry will not find it easy to resell its assets. Entry costs might therefore be irrecoverable.

(e) There are several reasons why newspaper publishers might seek to diversify into other media. One obvious reason is simply the desire to diversify and spread the risks of production. Another reason is that ownership of other media might be very useful in promoting newspapers, especially if the controlling firm could promote its own newspapers at a competitive advantage. There is also the possibility that other media yield higher returns than newspapers. This is especially true of independent television through the sale of advertising.

Question 3

(a) In making production decisions, firms consider only the private costs of production. However, in some cases, there are externalities associated with production. These externalities affect individuals or the environment despite the fact that they might not necessarily consume the product. We are told in the extract that one of the chief causes of acid rain is the emission of sulphur dioxide into the environment from chimneys. When this sulphur dioxide comes back to earth in the form of acid rain, it pollutes rivers and lakes, with the result that their recreational use – particularly for fishing, since fish die – diminishes. Similarly, it is responsible for the death of large numbers of trees and has caused extensive damage to forests. In a free market, this environmental cost is not borne directly by producers or consumers but by those people who lose access to an amenity.

(b) A pollution tax would raise the costs of production for the electricity generating companies. As a result, the price of the product would rise and consumption would fall by an amount which depends on the elasticity of demand. This is one way of reducing environmental pollution, and to achieve the optimal rate of pollution the tax should be set equal to the marginal social cost of production: that is, the private cost plus externalities. Figure TP4 shows the effect of a pollution tax on price and consumption of a product.

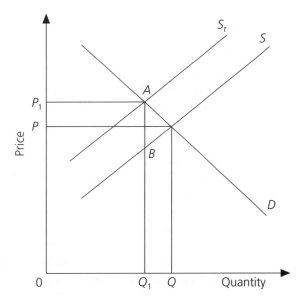

Figure TP4 The effect of a pollution tax on price and quantity

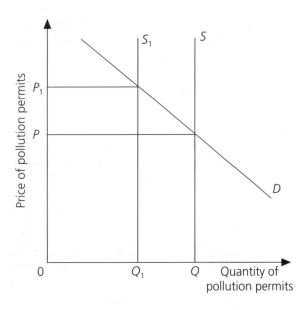

Figure TP5 The effect of a reduction in the supply of pollution permits on their price

In Figure TP4, *D* and *S* are the original demand and supply curves for this product. The equilibrium price and quantity are *P* and *Q* respectively. If a pollution tax equal to *AB* is imposed on this product, the supply curve shifts to S_t and, as a consequence, the equilibrium price rises to P_1 and the equilibrium quantity falls to Q_1.

(c) We are told in the extract that most of the pollution permits are initially to be given away free to polluters. Now, if the implied pollution quotas are equal to the existing rate of pollution, it might seem that firms have no incentive to cut back on the level of pollution they generate. However, we are also told that the number of pollution permits issued is to be reduced in future years and that they are to be auctioned. This gives firms a chance now to invest in pollution-reducing technologies and, in the absence of such investment, they will be compelled to reduce production (so as to cut back on pollution) or to purchase permits at the auction, thus raising their costs of production. As costs and prices rise for those firms compelled to purchase pollution permits, consumer demand will shift to the more efficient firms who generate less pollution. Figure TP5 is used to explain the effect of this on the price of pollution permits.

In Figure TP5, *D* and *S* are the original demand and supply curves for this product. The equilibrium price and quantity are *P* and *Q* respectively. Note that the supply of pollution permits is completely inelastic because they are issued by the government and cannot be 'manufactured' by firms. As the government reduces the supply of pollution permits, for example to S_1, the price of the permits is forced up as they are auctioned to the highest bidder. In this case, the effect of the reduction in supply is to force price up to P_1.

(d) Whether or not a firm decides to change its technology so as to generate less pollution from its production process depends on several factors. One important factor might be public pressure. If the activities of polluting firms are given media coverage, consumers might turn to other, cleaner products.

Another factor that might encourage firms to invest in cleaner technologies is the cost of such technologies compared with the expected cost of permits. If additional investment in more efficient cleaner production techniques is below the expected cost of the permits when they are auctioned, then firms have a clear incentive to invest in such techniques to avoid the necessity of buying permits. In reality, this is unlikely to be the case for all firms, and only the more efficient firms will be able to invest in the cleaner technologies.

Firms will also need to consider the likely future demand for their product. For the electricity generators this is not easy, since power stations have a relatively long life but demand might fall as buildings become better insulated and other forms of electricity generation, such as solar and wind power, become more economically viable because of changes in technology. If power stations take the view that demand for their product is likely to fall, the least efficient generators might choose to pay for pollution permits, rather than invest in new technology.

Question 4

Despite the existence of equal pay legislation in the UK, gender differentials exist with respect to pay, and in 1992, average female earnings were just over 70 per cent of average male earnings. There are two broad reasons for this: one is clearly the existence of some form of discrimination, and the other is that there are genuine differences between male and female workers.

Employers might discriminate in favour of male workers simply because they have an irrational preference for male workers over female workers. On the other hand, employers might discriminate against female workers because of the absence of perfect information about female applicants for particular jobs. Women are statistically more likely to drop out of the labour market (temporarily or permanently) than male workers. Whatever the source of discrimination, if employers have a preference for male workers over female workers, this might only be overcome if female workers accept lower pay. This scenario is analysed in terms of Figure TP6. In this figure, panel (a) shows the demand and supply conditions for male workers in a particular labour market. (The demand for male workers is based on their marginal revenue productivity.) The equilibrium wage rate is W_m and the number of male workers employed is N_m. Panel (b) of Figure TP6 shows the demand and supply conditions for female workers in the same

(a)   (b)

Figure TP6 The effect of discrimination on male and female wage rates and numbers employed

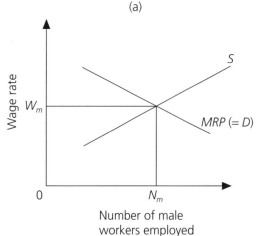

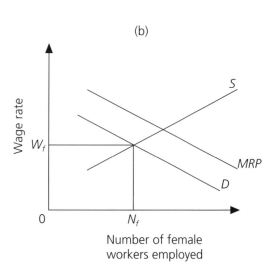

occupation as male workers. The equilibrium wage rate for female workers in W_f and the number of female workers employed is N_f. For purposes of analysis it is assumed that the supply and marginal revenue product conditions for female workers are identical to those for male workers.

Now, in a perfect market both groups would receive the same pay and the same numbers would be employed. However, when employers discriminate against female workers this is not the case and therefore the marginal revenue product for female workers is *not* the demand curve for female workers as it is for male workers. Instead, at any point on the marginal revenue product curve, employers will hire fewer women than if they did not discriminate. The actual demand curve for female employment therefore lies *below* the marginal revenue product curve for female workers. In terms of Figure TP6 this results in a wage of W_f with N_f female workers being employed, both wage and employment being *below* what they would otherwise have been.

In the UK, the Sex Discrimination Act is designed to prevent this type of discrimination. However, the legislation is not always easy to enforce since it is often difficult to establish conclusively that discrimination exists. Thus to the extent that it does exist, female workers who are unable to obtain employment at the same rate of pay as their male counterparts are compelled to seek employment in occupations where discrimination does not exist. This has a knock-on effect which further depresses average female earnings below those of average male workers because of the increased supply of female workers to such occupations. This no doubt partly explains the observed disproportionate representation of women in lower-paid occupations in the UK.

Discrimination might be the result of worker attitudes. For example, it is possible that male workers might not find the appointment of a female supervisor as acceptable as the appointment of a male supervisor. Hence should an employer appoint a female supervisor in these circumstances and the employees then refuse to give her their full cooperation, the consequence would almost certainly be that the productivity of the female supervisor will be less than the productivity of a male supervisor. If employers perceive male workers to have a higher productivity than female workers, this would partly account for differences in the average pay of both groups, since it would explain why female workers are underrepresented in the better-paid, more senior positions within firms.

It seems probable that average wage differentials between male and female workers are at least partly explained by discrimination. However, it is equally apparent that average wage differentials are also explained in part by differences in male/female characteristics and, in particular, by differences in human capital. Human capital refers to the accumulated education, skills and experience a person possesses. The greater the amount of human capital a worker possesses, the greater the pay likely to be earned by that worker.

Human capital is accumulated over time, and so the supply of workers who possess human capital is both lower and less elastic than the supply of workers who do not possess human capital. Similarly, the demand for workers who possess a relatively large amount of human capital is less elastic than the demand for workers who possess relatively little human capital, because of the greater difficulty in obtaining substitutes for skilled workers. Accordingly, if female workers on average possess less human capital than male workers, this will be reflected in lower average pay for female employees. *To the extent* that, on average, female workers possess less human capital than male workers, Figure TP7 demonstrates the impact on average levels of pay, where D_s and S_s show the demand and supply conditions for skilled workers and D_u and S_u show the demand and supply conditions for unskilled workers. The different demand and supply conditions explain the higher pay (W_s) of skilled workers compared with the lower pay (W_u) of unskilled workers.

It is well known that skilled workers receive on average more than unskilled workers, but as an explanation of differences in male/female average earnings this

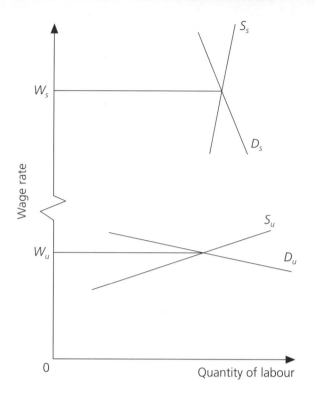

Figure TP7 The market for skilled and unskilled workers

raises the whole question of why female workers might possess less human capital than male workers. There might be several reasons for this.

It has already been implicitly alleged that one reason might be discrimination on the part of employers. Because of the greater incidence of females dropping out of the labour market than males, employers might be less willing to invest in training female workers than male workers. However, it is also true that, despite changing attitudes towards family roles, there remain differences in the extent to which male and female workers acquire human capital. On average, women spend more of their working lives on family matters and are therefore on average less likely to acquire the same amount of human capital as male workers. To the extent that this is correct, female workers will be compelled to seek employment in those sectors where human capital is less important. Again this would explain the overrepresentation of female workers in low-paid occupations such as ancillary work, hotel work and catering.

ANSWERS TO TIMED PRACTICE PAPER 2

Question 1

(a) (i) From mid-1987 until about the end of 1990, average earnings and inflation both tended to rise. However, the situation was reversed between the end of 1990 and the end of 1993 when they both tended to fall. In general, average earnings kept ahead of inflation.

(ii) The difference between average earnings and inflation was greater at the beginning of the period than at the end of the period, implying that over the whole of the period, real earnings, and therefore living standards, were higher at the beginning of the period than at the end of the period.

(b) (i) Unit labour costs follow the same basic pattern as average earnings. They rise and fall over the cycle. This is what might be expected since about 70 per cent of total costs in the UK consists of labour costs. However, it is not necessarily true that unit labour costs will rise simply because average earnings rise because of productivity increases. We are told that 'Some commentators argue that pay rises cause no significant problem if they are equal to any increase in labour productivity'.

(ii) However, to the extent that increases in average earnings are not matched by increases in productivity, unit labour costs will rise. It does not necessarily follow that this will fuel inflation. After all, employers might be willing to absorb increased costs through a cut in profits, especially because price changes also add to costs. Additionally, if demand for the product is elastic, a rise in price will lead to a disproportionately large reduction in sales. To avoid this, employers might feel compelled to absorb the increase in unit labour costs rather than face the consequences of higher prices.

(c) One of the main problems of government restrictions on pay rises is that it implies interfering with the price mechanism. Changes in wage differentials lead to changes in the allocation of labour to different industries. In particular, when demand for different goods and services increases it is only possible to respond to the increase in demand if additional resources, including labour, can be acquired. In other words, firms rely on increases in wage rates to recruit additional workers. In the absence of a change in the structure of wages because of government restrictions, this will happen at a much slower rate.

Another problem with government restrictions on wage rises is that once the restrictions are lifted, as they inevitably must be to remove labour market distortions, there tends to be a 'catching up' phase when labour unions attempt to make up the wage rises prohibited when the restrictions were in force. This will result either in increased inflationary pressure or in rising unemployment if the government implements measures to restrain demand. The history of restrictions on wage increases is that they fail to restrain wage costs over any sustainable period of time.

(d) If wage increases exceed the underlying increase in productivity, unit labour costs will rise. If firms are unable (or unwilling) to absorb the increase in unit labour costs, prices will rise. As previously indicated, labour costs account for about 70 per cent of total costs in the UK. So, for example, if unit labour costs rise by, say, 5 per cent, this implies a rise in total unit costs of 3.5 per cent. This has serious implications for the competitiveness of UK products **if costs are rising by a smaller amount** in the economies of our chief competitors.

This is particularly important in the UK at the present time because of the strength of sterling on the foreign exchange market. The rising value of the pound against other currencies adversely affects competitiveness since it increases the cost of exports and reduces the price of imports, making them more competitive in the domestic economy.

Question 2

(a) Exchange rates are the price of two monies, and in a free market the exchange rate between any pair of currencies is determined by supply and demand for those currencies. Sometimes governments intervene to influence the value of the exchange rate by sales and purchases of currency on the foreign exchanges and by adjusting the rate of interest so as to attract/reduce capital inflows and outflows.

Any adjustment in the exchange value of a country's currency changes the **foreign price of exports** (and the **domestic price of imports**). Take an initial exchange rate of £1 = \$1.55. A good which is produced in the UK and is sold at a domestic price of £2,000, has a dollar export price of \$3,100. If sterling now rises against the dollar, say to £1 = \$1.65, each unit of sterling now buys more dollars: that is, more dollars must be given up to buy the same quantity of sterling. The appreciation of sterling has no direct effect on the price of domestically produced output, but the dollar price is affected and in this case rises to \$3,300. The **value** of exports therefore rises when the exchange rate appreciates and, for the opposite reasons, declines when the exchange rate depreciates.

The effect of changes in the exchange rate on the **volume** of UK exports is less certain and depends partly on the elasticity of demand for exports. If demand is elastic then, following a rise in price caused by appreciation, total earnings from exports will fall. This is because the percentage reduction in quantity sold will be greater than the percentage rise in price. In other words, the rise in price has a relatively large effect on quantity sold. Exactly the opposite happens when demand for exports is inelastic. Total earnings from exports rise after appreciation because the rise in price has a relatively small impact on quantity sold.

Even if demand for UK exports is elastic, it does not follow that a change in the exchange rate will change either the volume or the value of exports. One distinct possibility is that firms will either cut the price of exports in domestic currency so as to preserve the pre-appreciation price or increase the price in domestic currency so as to preserve the pre-depreciation price of exports. Using the exchange rates quoted above, we have an export from the UK with a sterling price of £2,000, a pre-appreciation price of $3,100 and post-appreciation price of $3,300. If, after sterling appreciates, UK suppliers reduce the sterling price of the export to £1,878.80, the pre-appreciation dollar price is maintained at $3,100. Firms might very well adopt this policy and accept a small cut in profits so as to preserve market share. In the case of depreciation, a rise in the domestic price is necessary to preserve the pre-depreciation dollar price of exports. Again, firms might adopt this policy so as to avoid foreign firms retaliating to a price cut and, in any case, by increasing the sterling price they automatically increase their profits. If price changes are administered in this way following a change in the exchange rate, then neither the foreign currency value nor the volume of exports will change as exchange rates change.

Another relevant factor is the elasticity of supply of exports in the case of an exchange rate depreciation. When sterling depreciates the foreign price of exports falls, but it takes time for patterns of production to change. Unless there is spare capacity in the economy, retooling and retraining will be necessary and this, combined with the time lag involved before patterns of consumption change, might lead to a deteriorating current account deficit *after* depreciation. Only over time, as the elasticity of demand and supply increase, is there any real prospect of an increase in the value and volume of exports. Exactly the opposite reasoning tells us why export volume and value might initially increase after an appreciation of sterling.

A change in the exchange rate also has implications for domestic inflation in a country such as the UK, with its relatively high dependency on imports of raw materials. Take an appreciation of sterling from £1 = $1.55 to £1 = $1.65, and an import which sells at an international price of $5,000. Before sterling's appreciation this good would have cost £3225.81 in the UK. However, after sterling's appreciation, the **international price** of the good is unaffected but it now costs £3030.30 in the UK. This implies that imported raw materials become cheaper and, to the extent that imported raw materials are used in the production of exports, the lower cost of production might lead to increased sales. If demand is elastic, the value of exports will also rise and vice versa.

(b) So far, we have only considered the price of exports as determining export volume and value. In reality, there are many other factors that exert an influence on sales of exports. One important factor is the rate of inflation in the UK compared with the rate of inflation in overseas markets. If the rate of inflation is lower in the UK than in overseas markets, UK goods will become more competitive in world markets and this will have a favourable impact on UK exports.

Another factor is changes in productivity and unit labour costs in the UK compared with overseas producers. In recent years, productivity growth has been relatively high in the UK and wage increases have compared favourably with several other countries. The combined effect has been to reduce unit labour costs in the UK compared with many other countries, and this has favourably affected UK export performance.

A factor that has a significant impact on exports from any country is the level of economic activity in countries which are the main export markets. If economic activity is depressed or the rate of economic growth is sluggish, exports will not be as significant as they otherwise might be. The recent recession in many European countries that are the main destinations for UK exports might have had an adverse effect on the value and volume of those exports.

There are also non-price factors that affect the value and volume of UK exports. Traditionally, it has been alleged that UK products have a poorer reputation for design, delivery, reliability and after-sales service than products from other countries such as Germany and Japan. To the extent that this is true, it has obvious implications for UK export sales. Similarly, the extent of technological progress on which the development of new products sometimes depends is a crucial factor in affecting export performance in some sectors. Again, to the extent that other countries have an advantage over UK producers in this respect, export performance will be hampered.

In some cases there seems little doubt that UK export sales have been hampered by barriers to entry into overseas markets. Some countries have tariffs against exports from EU countries generally and this reduces UK exports below their potential levels. In other cases there are 'invisible barriers', such as unreasonably stringent safety regulations or excessive administrative procedures to be followed before goods from other countries are allowed into domestic markets. Again, to the extent that such barriers exist for UK producers, exports from the UK will be less than their potential levels.

Question 3

(a) Money is an extremely difficult concept to define, and it is usual for anything that performs the functions of money to be regarded as money. However, for policy purposes, a much more rigid definition of money is necessary. In recent years in the UK, the authorities have taken the view that no single measure of money can fully describe monetary conditions, and the distinction between broad money and narrow money is important because they provide different indicators of the state of the financial system. Narrow money in the UK is measured by M0, which is simply notes and coins in circulation (including the amount in banks' tills) and operational deposits held at the Bank of England. This is the most liquid measure of money in the UK, but it is considered by many to be of little practical value since it gives no indication of spending potential in the economy. Broad money is currently measured by M4, and the main components of this aggregate are sight and time deposits placed with recognized financial institutions. Changes in this measure of broad money are now considered by many to give a better guide to changes in the future rate of inflation.

(b) The effect of an increase in the money supply on prices, output and employment depends partly on whether we consider an increase in broad money or an increase in narrow money. It is possible for the narrow money supply to increase and simply be absorbed into banks' till money, in which case it is possible that there will be no significant effect on any of the macroeconomic variables mentioned. It is therefore better to consider that the increase in the money supply is an increase in broad money.

In this case, an increase in the money supply implies an increase in aggregate demand. After all, if the money supply goes up, some economic agents will be holding more money than they desire at the ruling price level and, as a consequence, they will increase their spending. The initial effect of the increase in aggregate demand is shown in Figure TP8, where AD_0 is the initial aggregate demand curve and AS_{s0} is the initial short-run aggregate supply curve. Aggregate demand varies inversely with the price level because, as prices fall, the purchasing power of money rises and hence a greater volume of output is demanded. Aggregate supply varies directly with the price level because, as prices rise, firms

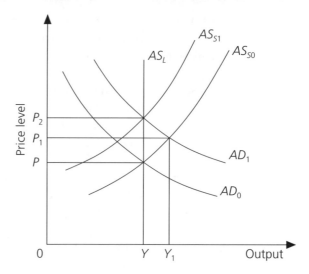

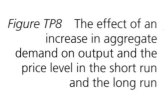

Figure TP8 The effect of an
increase in aggregate
demand on output and the
price level in the short run
and the long run

can still produce profitably despite the existence of rising costs caused by
diminishing returns. Given the aggregate demand and aggregate supply curve
above, P is the equilibrium price and Y is the equilibrium level of national income.

The quantity theory of money is widely regarded as the best predictor of the
effect of an increase in the money supply on the price level. The income version
of the equation of exchange from which the quantity theory is derived can be
written as:

$$MV_Y = PY$$

where:

M = some measure of the money supply;
V_Y = the income velocity of circulation: that is, the average number of times
the money supply is used to purchase final output;
P = the average price level for final output; and
Y = real income: that is, the volume of final output.

It is assumed that V_Y and Y are constant in the long run or at least change so
slowly that for simplicity they can be treated as constant in the long run. This fact
implies that both V_Y and Y are determined by institutional factors and are not
influenced by changes in the money supply. Because Y is constant in the long run,
the long-run aggregate supply curve is vertical and the level of output at which
supply is perfectly inelastic is known as the natural rate.

However, while Y and V_Y might be constant in the long run, they might exhibit
considerable short-run variability. Because of this, an increase in aggregate
demand – in this case, caused by an expansion of the money supply – leads
initially to an increase in output as the economy moves up the short-run aggregate
supply curve AS_{S0}. Any increase in aggregate supply also implies an increase in
employment.

In Figure TP8, AD_1 represents the increase in aggregate demand. Output rises
to Y_1 and therefore employment also rises but, because aggregate supply is not
perfectly elastic, the price level also rises, in this case to P_1. However, this is only a
partial equilibrium and, when wage rates are renegotiated, costs of production
will rise and this will shift the short-run aggregate supply curve to AS_{S1}. Long-run
equilibrium is established when the price level has risen to P_2, output has returned
to its natural rate Y, and therefore employment also reverts to the natural rate.

Note that as the aggregate supply curve shifts to AS_{S1}, aggregate demand
contracts along the curve AD_1. This contraction of aggregate demand is, of course,
partly because the real value of money balances falls as the price level rises.
However, it is also true that any rise in the price level will pull up the nominal rate

of interest so as to preserve the real rate of interest. The rise in interest rates will result in a fall in the rate of investment, and this provides a further reason why aggregate demand will contract.

The effect of an increase in the money supply is therefore to increase prices, output and employment in the short run, but to increase only prices in the long run.

Question 4

The standard of living is usually measured by per capita income or GNP per head. To the extent that the standard of living depends on the amount of output available for consumption, comparing per capita income in different countries might provide a guide to relative standards of living.

However, the standard of living is an elusive concept and depends on many factors, rather than simply on GNP per head. It depends on levels of literacy, life expectancy, the degree of political freedom, the amount of leisure time available, the extent of negative externalities such as pollution and so on. If these factors differ between countries, then simple comparisons of per capita income will give a misleading indication of relative living standards.

Another reason why it might be inappropriate to compare relative per capita income as a guide to relative living standards is that the standard of living is not simply determined by average income per head, it is also determined by the **distribution of income**. If the distribution is relatively even in a country, per capita income will more accurately reflect the standard of living in that country than when the distribution of income is relatively uneven. If there are differences in the distribution of income between countries, simply comparing per capita income will give a misleading indication of the extent to which the standard of living of the **average** person differs between these countries.

In some cases, comparison of GNP per capita might give a misleading indication of relative living standards because there are differences in the composition of GNP. For example, some countries spend more on defence than other countries. Such expenditure does not add directly to the standard of living, and the opportunity cost of increased defence expenditure might be lower production of consumer goods. Similarly, greater investment implies less output for immediate consumption. In both cases, simply comparing per capita incomes in different countries will not accurately reflect relative standards of living.

Some countries have climatic advantages, so that they can enjoy heating and lighting as gifts of nature and therefore need to devote fewer resources to these activities. In other countries, where heating and lighting is not so freely available, it must be produced from scarce resources, and again the opportunity cost might be lower output of goods for immediate consumption. Here also per capita income would not be a reliable guide to relative standards of living in different countries.

In some countries, per capita income is high relative to domestic consumption. The most obvious example of this is many of the OPEC countries which export oil but do not consume an equivalent amount of imports. In other words, they have a surplus on their current accounts. On the other side of the coin, by running a current account deficit a country can consume a greater amount than it currently produces and so can enjoy a standard of living greater than might be expected, given its per capita income.

One feature of all economies is the existence of an underground or hidden economy: that is, in order to evade taxation, productive activities which are liable to taxation are undisclosed to the authorities. While the underground economy exists in all economies, its magnitude might vary considerably between countries. When there is significant variation in the size of the underground economy, simple comparisons of per capita income will again be unreliable as a guide to relative standards of living.

For purposes of comparison, per capita incomes are converted into US dollars, using **purchasing power parities**. This is regarded as the most reliable method of establishing a common currency but, to the extent that purchasing power parities fail to reflect actual purchasing power in different countries, comparisons of per capita income will not provide a suitable basis for comparing actual standards of living in different countries.

Despite its limitations, per capita income is still the most widely used measure of the standard of living, and the limitations noted above do not necessarily imply that per capita income provides an unacceptable basis for comparing the standard of living in different countries. However, these limitations do imply that comparisons based on per capita income must be interpreted with caution and should perhaps be supplemented with other indicators of the standard of living, such as the number of cars per head of population, life expectancy, standards of nutrition, and so on. For all these reasons, simple comparisons of per capita income might not be suitable for measuring relative standards of living.

LONGMAN
EXAM
PRACTICE
KITS

REVISION
PLANNER

Getting Started — *Begin on week 12*

Use a calendar to put dates onto your planner and write in the dates of your exams. Fill in your targets for each day. Be realistic when setting the targets, and try your best to stick to them. If you miss a revision period, remember to re-schedule it for another time.

Get Familiar — *Weeks 12 and 11*

Identify the topics on your syllabuses. Get to know the format of the papers – time, number of questions, types of questions. Start reading through your class notes, coursework, etc.

Get Serious — *Week 10*

Complete reading through your notes – you should now have an overview of the whole syllabus. Choose 12 topics to study in greater depth for each subject. Allocate two topic areas for each subject for each of the next 6 weeks

No. of weeks before the exams	Date: Week commencing	MONDAY	TUESDAY
12			
11			
10			

WEDNESDAY	THURSDAY	FRIDAY	SATURDAY	SUNDAY

No. of weeks before the exams	Date: Week commencing	MONDAY	TUESDAY
9			
8			
7			
6			
5			
4			
3			
2			
1			

Get Revising · Weeks 9 to 4

Working on the basis of covering two topics per week an ideal pattern to follow for each week would be:

Read through your class notes and coursework.

Summarise the main points:

- write down the main principles/theories
- outline key terms and definitions
- note important examples/illustrations
- list important data/formula

(Using a highlighter pen is very useful here)

Practise answering exam questions:

- work through the questions in your Longman Exam Practice Kits
- write outline answers
- write full answers to some questions giving yourself the same time as in the exam
- make sure that you try to answer questions of each type set in the exam
- check your answers with those provided in your Longman Exam Practice Kit. Learn from any mistakes you have made.

Get Confidence · Weeks 3 to 1

➤ Have a final read through of all your class notes and coursework.
➤ Read through the summaries you have already made.
➤ Try to reduce these summary notes to a single side of A4 paper.
➤ Test yourself to check that you can remember everything on each A4 page.
➤ Go over the practice questions already attempted.

The day before the exams

➤ Read through each A4 summary sheet.
➤ Check that you have all the equipment you need for the exam.
➤ Do something you enjoy in the evening.
➤ Go to bed reasonably early: tired students rarely give their best.

The exam – get up and go

➤ Have a good breakfast to give you energy.
➤ Don't panic – everyone else is nervous too.
➤ Remember – the examiners are looking for opportunities to give you marks, not take them away!

Good luck!

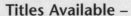

Titles Available –

GCSE
Biology
Business Studies
Chemistry
English
French
Geography
German
Higher Maths
Information
Systems
Mathematics
Physics
Science

A-LEVEL
Biology
British and European
  Modern History
Business Studies
Chemistry
Economics
French
Geography
German
Mathematics
Physics
Psychology
Sociology

There are lots of ways to revise. It is important to find what works best for you. Here are some suggestions:

- try testing with a friend: testing each other can be fun!
- label or highlight sections of text and make a checklist of these items.
- learn to write summaries – these will be useful for revision later.
- try reading out loud to yourself.
- don't overdo it – the most effective continuous revision session is probably between forty and sixty minutes long.
- practise answering past exam papers and test yourself using the same amount of time as you will have on the actual day – this will help to make the exam itself less daunting.
- pace yourself, taking it step by step.

WEDNESDAY	THURSDAY	FRIDAY	SATURDAY	SUNDAY

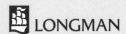